THE RISE OF THE TRANSCENDENCE LEADER-COACH

Ihab Badawi

You will not be the same leader by the time you finish this book.

Decoding Human-Centric Leadership

THE RISE OF THE TRANSCENDENCE LEADER-COACH

A Unique Framework for Extraordinary Leadership

Transform Your Leadership with 6 Mindset Pillars and 16 Competencies of the Transcendence Leader-Coach

Ihab Badawi

The Rise of the Transcendence Leader-Coach
Copyright © 2024 Ihab Badawi
First published in 2024

Print: 978-1-76124-094-2
E-book: 978-1-76124-097-3
Hardback: 978-1-76124-096-6

All rights reserved. No part of this book may be reproduced, stored in a retrieval system, or transmitted by any means (electronic, mechanical, photo-copying, recording, or otherwise) without written permission from the author.

Because of the dynamic nature of the Internet, any web addresses or links contained in this book may have changed since publication and may no longer be valid. The information in this book is based on the author's experiences and opinions. The views expressed in this book are solely those of the author and do not necessarily reflect the views of the publisher; the publisher hereby disclaims any responsibility for them.

The author of this book does not dispense any form of medical, legal, financial, or technical advice either directly or indirectly. The intent of the author is solely to provide information of a general nature to help you in your quest for personal development and growth. In the event you use any of the information in this book, the author and the publisher assume no responsibility for your actions. If any form of expert assistance is required, the services of a competent professional should be sought.

Publishing information
Publishing and design facilitated by
Passionpreneur Publishing
A division of Passionpreneur Organization Pty Ltd
ABN: 48640637529

Melbourne, VIC | Australia
www.PassionpreneurPublishing.com

*To my beloved family for providing me with a
solid support system during this journey over the years;*

*To my parents for manifesting special traits of leadership which I
uncovered day after day providing a valuable benchmark to live by;*

*To my team, friends, and community members for their
positive energy and eagerness to learn;*

*To every leader I have met, to every person I have disagreed with,
and to every challenge I have faced:*

*You have all helped in crystalizing my
view of what true leadership is.*

Table of Contents

Acknowledgments	ix
Introduction	xi
Preface	xv
The Awakening	xvii

SECTION I   1

Chapter 1   The Transcendence Leader-Coach (TLC)   3
Chapter 2   The Vortex   11
Chapter 3   The Paradigm Shift   27
Chapter 4   Embracing the Coaching Approach   35
Chapter 5   The Conscious Leader-Coach   45

SECTION II   63

Chapter 6   The Transcendence Leader-Coach Mindset   67
Chapter 7   Building Bridges   101

Chapter 8 The Door to Fluid Leadership	121
Chapter 9 Service with a Sense of Purpose	143
Chapter 10 Trust is Everything	161
Chapter 11 Where Does True Leadership Start?	181
Conclusion	191
Some More Offerings	195
Author's Biography	197

Acknowledgments

Writing a book was harder than expected, and finishing the book was much more transformative than I could have imagined. None of this would have been possible without my team who supported and encouraged me all the way.

Thanks to Abir, Amani, Nadine, Randa, Hala, & Katya for being the core team who shaped the meaning of trust, commitment, and belief in a shared vision.

Introduction

> *"A leader takes people where they want to go.*
> *A great leader takes people where they don't*
> *necessarily want to go, but ought to be."*
>
> — ROSALYNN CARTER[1]

The fact that you intend to read this book is a testimony that you are committed to developing your leadership, and, for that, I acknowledge the self-learner in you.

This book provides the essential framework that every true leader should have to attain the desired results and enhance efficiency and profitability through creating an environment conducive to the growth and nurturing of future leaders.

It provides the blueprint for you to become a Neo-Leader to lead based on trust rather than power, to lead without a position. In the article "Why CEO's fail," written by Elena

Botelho and Kim Powell, published by Harvard Business[2], the authors discuss how CEOs fail due to a variety of factors, including their inability to cope with complexity and adapt to change. The authors suggest that CEOs who fail to adapt to changing circumstances and complexity often have a narrow focus and lack the flexibility needed to navigate complex challenges. They are unable to deal with the impact of the VUCA world (Volatility, Uncertainty, Complexity, and Ambiguity) on them, their teams, and the work environment.

Leaders need to generate a new level of awareness that enables them to see through these changes, lead behavioral change from within, and transcend cultural differences.

Imagine being able to attain a multi-dimensional awareness that facilitates your capacity to be grounded and resilient, with the capability to harness the collective wisdom of the team instead of resolving everything on your own: being a leader capable of creating an environment of creativity and innovation.

While reading this book, you will:

- Identify the real challenges that leaders face;
- Understand the six pillars for embracing the Leader-Coach mindset;
- Acquire the necessary steps to act on the 16 competencies of the Transcendence Leader-Coach; and
- Unlock the three keys to become a Transcendence Leader-Coach.

INTRODUCTION

During a long journey managing operations across 58 countries over 22 years, I had the chance to research the essence of leadership, understand the impact of culture and systems on leadership development, and, above all, identify the common pillars that can transcend the limits of cultures and formal systems. This fueled my passion to work with people like you and thus quit the corporate life and start working with various organizations across the globe to support them in shaping a new meaning of leadership from within.

Preface

A lot of literature has been written on leadership and more is yet to come as leadership continues to evolve and adapt to ever-changing dynamics. At such times, leaders need to re-envision themselves and check-in to see if they are evolving at the right speed to overcome the challenges and support those around them.

Some concepts may seem familiar to leaders; however, they will not seem applicable or even make sense until they are looked at as a complete picture, as a complete framework - The TLC framework. This is because they only complement each other when put in the right framework and based on the right mindset.

Through this book, I intend to support leaders to evolve and transcend into a new state from which they can lead with a deeper impact. This new leadership style will re-envision the organizational culture to become a culture of conversations and reshape the working environment to be one of engagement and fulfillment, leading to breakthrough innovations and higher efficiencies through embracing a new mindset capable of unlocking a new leadership approach that will galvanize those surrounding leaders. There are 6 pillars to this mindset that will unlock 16 unique competencies that will shape the leaders' future, teams, and organizations.

Leaders are facing new challenges, varying from the global economy to geopolitical shifts, pandemics, technology, and changing generational behaviors which lead to the dynamic complexity that we will unpack as we walk through the journey of the Transcendence Leader-Coach or the TLC.

The TLC is a Neo-Leader who can navigate a world of Volatility, Uncertainty, Complexity, and Ambiguity (the VUCA world) and who is capable of breeding new leaders with a more human-centric approach that generates more connection, alignment, and engagement: the factors for success in shaping the human behavior in organizations.

We shall decode the Humancentric leadership by unpacking the Transcendence Leader-Coach (TLC) framework through the subtle powers of coaching that lead to a culture of conversations which facilitate growth, and support in identifying the hidden potential of the greatest asset in the organization (its people) and expanding that potential through Connection, Versatility, Service, and Trust. And we shall outline how to overcome the barriers that usually limit leadership evolution.

The Awakening

> *"Sometimes all it takes is a simple push, a nudge that creates a ripple effect that will shape the future."*
>
> – IHAB BADAWI

Where Is MY Equity?

It all started with this question, which kicked off an awakening in me.

At the start of my career, I had the decision to choose between a better salary or connections. I was lucky to have the right mentor at that time (back in the days when it was rare to have a mentor) and I concluded at the end of the meeting, with my mentor, that it would be best to choose connections.

THE RISE OF THE TRANSCENDENCE LEADER-COACH

> *"The two vices of leadership: Ego and Fear. Leaders acting from their egos are blinded and they see through their ego filters. Leaders trapped in fear are driven by the fear of losing power, position, or even image which creates an environment of distrust, skepticism, and slow movement."*
>
> – IHAB BADAWI

It was a low-paid position yet a major door opener and a major learning gateway, I might add. I thought that taking that route would allow me to interact with the right top leaders in various industries. To my shock, it didn't. A young chap, career driven, was expecting to work with a leader who would lead the way, walk the talk, and provide support! Connections were great, but I was not exposed to the best leadership styles. On the contrary, my experience started with me dealing with various leadership styles that ranged from autocratic to egocentric. The more I dedicated myself to the organization, the more pressure I felt.

Fast-forward a few years and, moving up the ladder, I started understanding the reasons behind such leadership approaches. I call them the two vices of leadership: Ego and Fear. Leaders acting from their egos are blinded and they see through their ego filters. The result is judgment, defensiveness, and one-way communication. Leaders trapped in fear are driven by the fear of losing power, position, or even image which creates an environment of distrust, skepticism, and slow movement.

From leaders in each camp, there was no support or guidance. It was an "I know it all" environment. I came to a point where I had to decide whether to go with the flow or challenge myself and move on. Choosing the latter was the best choice for me to avoid the contagious effect. Another fast-forward and I was at the C-suite level at an international organization with a slightly different picture. I was now dealing with autocracy, and at that point, I thought the cure was an achievement; however, at a big price.

I have no complaints: it was an era of success and rewards, though it was draining. It was a time in which I created a legacy and left a mark in the industry, by expanding into new territories and reaching the 58 markets benchmark and managing a large cross-cultural team. It was the era of higher-level learning. Focusing on the achievements and sheltering the team from any pressure coming from the top led to some blind spots that, in turn, led me to miss reading the red flags appearing in other areas of the organization which manifested themselves in different ways.

The biggest cost I identified back then was seeing high-level managers starting to adopt the same autocratic approach within the organization, leading to silo management as this approach trickled down. While others adopted a silent approach, which lead to fear and covering backs, it was clear at that point that the environment was becoming toxic and major signs could be seen with good talents leaving the organization. The question was: what to do about it? Is this the environment to be in? Is this how leadership should be? How does it relate to the leadership style that I believe in and am abiding by with my team? Should I stay or should I leave?

Leave! What about my team? What about my achievements so far? What about all the time I have invested so far? What about the internal challenge?

It was clear that the way things were going was not healthy, yet too much was at stake: the team.

Believing in a higher set of values, I chose to challenge the status quo and the environment around me. I succeeded with the immediate circle and failed dismally with the outer circle, with some peers, and definitely with the top leader, who was leading from a state of power. I tried my approach in various countries of our operation and interestingly succeeded in a few which caused me to start studying trends in leaders' personalities and organizational cultures.

Not moving with the speed of change that I hoped for, became depressing. Quitting was always an option for me when I took into consideration the price I was paying - being totally consumed with work, not spending enough time with family and friends, not having a healthy lifestyle, and working long hours - yet quitting in defeat was never a consideration.

THE AWAKENING

I started reflecting on all the experiences I've had while operating in various regions: The Middle East, Africa, the Indian Subcontinent, ASEAN, China, Europe, and North America. I started reflecting on the successes we had had in some areas where we initiated change. I started noticing certain similarities which made the change more applicable. It was a set of traits unique to each culture. It started to dawn on me that toxic leaders need a different approach to shift their mindset before their behavior. I started noticing that many lessons learned from various cultures can actually support the change process if put together in a way that facilitates growth within each unique environment. The solution was starting to form based on what I was applying with my team, though it was not crystal clear yet.

The wake-up call did not come until one day when one of the senior chiefs stepped into my office as I was celebrating a recent success with my team over the phone in another continent. He was fully demoralized and defeated, asking "Where is my equity?" He kept repeating the statement over and over again: "Where is my equity? Where is my equity?"

This statement struck a chord in me. At that time, I was focused on the vision I had set as a young man and was totally single-minded in wanting to challenge the current management approach in the organization. Little did I know, at that moment, that this would lead me to research a new path for leadership, that would lead me, a few years later, to have a complete career shift and expand my success to levels I had never considered.

It was that question, "Where is my equity?" that led to this. It was asked by a senior chief executive who had just come out of a heated meeting with the CEO, where he was blamed and insulted in front of his regional team for something he had nothing to do with, after a 15-year record of successes.

That incident triggered me to start a questioning process of my own:

- What is corporate equity for corporate leaders (not organizational equity)?
- What is my equity?
- What is the value of stability and sustainability?
- What is the resulting cost of bad leadership on the organization as a whole: loss of efficiency, high attrition rate (people leaving), draining of skills, higher cost of recruitment, or higher cost of training and development?
- Above all, what is the impact on the team: lack of motivation, loss of creativity, or reduced initiative?

That pushed me to focus my research on leadership in 58 countries and analyze the most effective leadership characteristics that would make the best leader.

> *"Become the type of leader that people would follow voluntarily, even if you had no title or position."*
>
> – BRIAN TRACY

My mission became to find a leader who could lead without a position or a need for power. And it was there that I found the power of coaching.

> *"Look at adversity through a lens of opportunity."*
>
> — IHAB BADAWI

I have learned many lessons in various countries and seen some common learnings in specific regions which have supported me to shape the TLC framework.

In the Middle East, I learned the caring parental type of leadership, where a leader takes care of his team as part of his family, and I studied the implementation of that leadership approach. And so, just as in different areas this approach can be having a positive impact on the work environment, the misalignment or misrepresentation of this leadership approach can be harmful to the organization. Looking at the positive aspects and the lessons I can draw from that parental approach reflects a kind of nurturing leadership style or approach which supports or creates safety for that team to stand on their own feet while knowing that somebody has their back.

In Africa, I learned the power of grit, maintaining course no matter what the challenges are, maintaining focus toward the objective, and having an orientation of continuing until that objective is achieved. This spilled-over confidence to the team and a belief that being committed will yield success.

THE RISE OF THE TRANSCENDENCE LEADER-COACH

In India, I encountered a new leadership approach based on authentic service, and how to lead a community and an organization by being of authentic service to others. This was a different leadership approach; an approach that gains power by serving others. This is where the concept of "to lead is to serve" was ingrained in my mindset. Spending around seven years managing different operations in India allowed me to experience how the concept of authentic service can be put in place to bring power. Serving others brings about humility and reflects power through respect. It attracts people to follow a leader based on gratitude, respect, and loyalty.

In Asia, I was able to see how people lead from their hearts with compassion. By studying compassion and how it can impact other people, I was able to see how compassion is interwoven with empathy and that leading from the heart does not mean being soft or weak. It means being able not only to listen with your mind, but also with your heart, to create deeper connections based on understanding, meaning, and context, and to appreciate differences rather than judging them.

When I moved to managing operations in China, I learned to lead with resilience; bouncing back no matter what I faced. I saw how leaders instilled resilience in others, whatever failures and challenges they might face, they can bounce back, stand on their own feet, and adapt as they evolve, which I liked most about the concept of leadership based on resilience. That was a key concept that shifted the way I thought at that point. It's not about adapting to the changes around you but embracing

THE AWAKENING

those changes so that you can evolve and accommodate those changes and put them in service of moving forward.

In Europe, the experience I had in different European countries shaped my concept of diversity as I looked at how leaders in Europe accept and embrace diverse cultures and build on that diversity. I saw how leaders perceive diversity as an empowering zone, as an empowering platform on which they are able to build. They can color their approach, strategies, and management style by allowing different people and different cultures to contribute to a collective leadership approach.

In North America, what I was able to draw from various leaders I dealt with is the focus on growth through inclusion. And inclusion means opening up a fair chance for everyone to contribute by invitation. I personally saw it as an "inviting leadership," a leadership approach that is all based on inviting others to chip-in, and have the chance to say, share, and partake no matter how small their contribution is.

> *It's not about adapting to the changes around you but embracing those changes so that you can evolve and accommodate those changes and put them in service of moving forward.*

I always wondered how to connect all these key learnings from all these cultures. As I started my coaching journey to support my team, I started discovering that coaching embraced all the key characteristics of successful leadership that I have learned across the continents. It was the missing piece that could remodel the current leadership. Thus, embracing The Transcendence Leader-Coach (TLC) approach was the way forward, coaching upwards, sideways, and downwards. The solution was to create a coaching culture, a culture of conversations that would eventually attract all stakeholders and increase the number of positive catalysts of change. I noticed that this required a process, a model, or a framework to hold it all together. And so, this led to the development of a new leadership framework: The Transcendence Leader-Coach (TLC).

It was not about coaching the team to shield them and build a departmental environment that was conducive to success and preparing the ground for new leaders, but about elevating them to become Transcendence Leader-Coaches themselves capable of leading self and others (their team, peers, and management).

As I started to apply this framework, while constantly shaping it, an environment of open communication started to grow across the organizations as those new leaders started opening up more to other departments and destroying silos. Coaching became a way of life within the organization and at a personal level.

The results were obvious: empathetic communication and curious authentic inquiry led to alignment and helped people get on the same page. This led to better efficiencies as goals were aligned, plans were streamlined, and differences were resolved. What was more important was that it led to more engagement, as more and more team members started to get involved because they were now being heard. The Leader-Coaches were listeners who listened most of the time and inquired from a place of positive curiosity, as a coach would do, as they were genuinely interested in what others had to share. People started going the extra mile, and more and more people were now motivated to take the opportunity and initiative to rise to the occasion.

Productivity reached an all-time high, efficiency rates were up, even major savings were recorded at high rates and operations expanded to new territories. We started attracting teams from big conglomerates as the news of this work environment transformation traveled.

Embracing the TLC approach consolidated my learnings about leadership and opened a new door to research and experimentation further across 58 countries to see how we could learn from the successful application of the model in different cultures and monitor its effectiveness.

My focus was to test and see if the new approach would yield better results than before in areas we found difficulty, and what we could learn from various cultures' approaches, and weave those learnings into the TLC path.

While I was focusing on transforming the organization, I was starting my path to coaching mastery. So, not only I was researching the best practices in 58 countries, but I was actually researching coaching as a field in depth to understand its dynamics and how it could result in sustainable impact.

My passion for coaching grew, as I saw its impact over and over again. This is when I started to feel that my calling in life was to support many organizations, rather than being a part of just one. I felt a growing obligation to support the many people out there who are suffering in weak or toxic work environments, to transform their organizations into successful, thriving places. And thus, the TLC Framework was my way to supporting other organizations and true leaders.

On my path to coaching mastery, I have studied and researched various coaching models to find the best approach to help leaders transform themselves and the environment around them, starting with myself. This led me to develop the Transcendence Coaching Model first, and from there develop the TLC framework. Of course, it would not be possible to cover the whole realm of coaching in this book, but we will highlight what leaders require to become TLCs.

I decided to write this book to share key learnings and to support individuals and organizations with a leadership framework that embraces the TLC approach. I hope to support them to build an environment conducive to nurturing future leaders who are capable of facing the inevitable, continuous challenges by embracing a unique mindset and modeling the right set of competencies. This framework will act as a reminder of the main virtues of a true leader. This book will be a kind of guide for some of us who may have wandered off the track over the years, a reminder to return to the essence of true leadership that drives efficiency and growth while connecting to the essence of people.

The TLC framework is a human-centric approach to leadership that empowers team members, organizations, and society as a whole, rather than just empowering the leaders themselves. It is intended to be a reminder for all leaders to maintain a path that influences others through positive sustainable impact.

SECTION I

In the VUCA world, leaders face unprecedented challenges that require them to be agile, adaptable, and resilient. As a result, the traditional hierarchical leadership model is no longer effective. Leaders must embrace a human-centric leadership approach that values collaboration, transparency, and empathy. This means empowering team members to take ownership of their roles, recognizing their contributions, and fostering a culture of inclusivity.

Despite the need for a human-centric approach, many leaders are struggling to adapt to the changing landscape. They face challenges such as global competition, rapidly evolving technologies, and a diverse and remote workforce. They also have to navigate increasing levels of complexity and ambiguity while maintaining high levels of productivity and efficiency. These challenges require leaders to shift their mindset from a command-and-control model to one that is more collaborative and coach-like.

By adopting a coaching approach, leaders can leverage the collective wisdom of their team and foster a culture of continuous learning and improvement. This means becoming leader-coaches themselves, empowering their team members to take ownership of their work and helping them develop the skills and knowledge they need to thrive in the VUCA world. In the following chapters, we will explore in detail the concepts of human-centric leadership, the challenges leaders face in the VUCA world, and how coaching can help leaders make the necessary mindset shift to become more effective in this dynamic landscape.

> *By adopting a coaching approach, leaders can leverage the collective wisdom of their team and foster a culture of continuous learning and improvement.*

1

THE TRANSCENDENCE LEADER-COACH (TLC)

A Human-Centric Leadership Approach

"The challenge of leadership is to be strong but not rude, to be kind but not weak, to be humble, but not timid."

– JIM ROHN

Coaching and leadership are utterly intertwined. As the world constantly evolves, leaders face many changing dynamics that continuously drive and direct them to re-envision the way they show up to lead their teams and the way they are required to lead their organizations, societies, or families. Regardless of capacity, everyone is a leader and has an impact on others and the surrounding environment in one way or another. Unless they are conscious, intentional, and clear about the type of leadership they manifest, leaders will not be able to perceive the impact they create around them. And unless they intentionally identify the type of leadership approach to instill, to cope with the changes surrounding them, they will not be able to govern these impacting changes.

The Impact of Coaching

Leaders breed new leaders. It is at the core of leadership to develop others to grow and become leaders themselves, and coaching is what makes this core possible and empowers leaders to do so.

Coaching is all about supporting others to tap into their potential, explore the hidden potential, and evoke it from within. It allows them to maximize their potential by expanding their thinking capacity and perspective on things around them. Coaching unlocks people's creativity and insight to craft their own path toward what provides them the utmost fulfillment.

Coaches support in expanding people's horizons, help them look at matters from different perspectives, look at change and opportunities or challenges they are facing from different angles, and consider how they can create that internal self-control and self-management to embrace, rather than reject, whatever is facing them. This is in itself a major influence as it enables a shift of mindset for others, a paradigm shift.

John Whitmore, the father of professional coaching, identified coaching as:

> *"Helping people to learn rather than find their own solutions."*

If we explore the definition of coaching as defined by the International Coaching Federation (ICF):

"Coaching is partnering with clients in a thought-provoking and creative process that inspires them to maximize their personal and professional potential. It is an ongoing professional relationship that helps people produce fulfilling results in their lives, careers, businesses, or organizations."[3]

Some of the keywords here are "partnership," "thought-provoking," and "creative journey." It all starts by building a partnership based on equality and trust. During the coaching process, hierarchy fades, thus eliminating any wall that might block communication. Trust is at the heart of the partnership: trusting the capability of the coachee. This by itself is empowering to others and provides confidence as well as opening the door for the coachee to reciprocate this trust toward the coach (the leader when acting as a Leader-Coach). When working with a client, the coach's main concern is to encourage the client to start thinking with new horizons in mind while expanding their learning capacity. Likewise, when leaders give this chance and expand that learning capacity for their team and colleagues, they are offering them the chance to become more creative. However, if creativity is not reached, coaching unlocks the resourcefulness within others where they can expand and reach out to their support systems. Leaders who embrace coaching are able to establish a safe space for individuals to open up, share, contribute, explore with courage, and dive into areas without fearing being wrong. Such an environment eventually fosters more engagement.

Many organizations invest heavily in seeking to develop creativity and innovation without being aware that the solution is within their reach already: by uplifting the level of existing leadership within the organization and embracing a coaching approach, thereby embedding a coaching culture.

> *"When coaching becomes the leaders' custom,*
> *they create a culture of creativity and innovation."*
>
> *– IHAB BADAWI*

According to a study conducted by the ICF & The Human Capital Institute (HCI) 2016 – Building a Coaching Culture with Managers and Leaders - on the impact of coaching on teams & organizations:

THE TRANSCENDENCE LEADER-COACH (TLC)

What are the most important indicators of coaching impact that have been observed for the Individual/ Team/ Organization?

What are the most important indicators of coaching impact that have been observed for the Individual/ Team/ Organization?

FIGURE 1.1: ICF & THE HUMAN CAPITAL INSTITUTE (HCI) 2016 – BUILDING A COACHING CULTURE WITH MANAGERS AND LEADERS

- ❖ 57% reported improved team functioning;
- ❖ 56% reported increased engagement;
- ❖ 51% reported increased productivity;
- ❖ 45% reported improved employee relations; and
- ❖ 36% reported faster leadership development.

Empathy as a Main Prerequisite

Empathy is a prerequisite or a requirement for coaches to be effective. It is about understanding others, rather than diving into their situation. Empathy is not sympathy; it is listening objectively with no judgment. This is what makes coaching the highest level of communication, and an essential pillar in building high-performance teams in organizations.

The level of communication, the type of language, and the way people communicate create the culture within the organization. Similarly, in societies, the way people communicate their language and express themselves shapes their culture, and their culture shapes their future. The reason why we say coaching is the highest level of communication is because of its embedded characteristics that enable objective observation and judgment-free conversations.

Coaching is not only about powerful questions, as some might think. Coaching is 80% about empathetic listening which empowers both parties: the speaker and the listener. By embracing coaching, coaches are building a culture where they listen, appreciate, and understand rather than listen to formulate arguments. The conversation shifts from being a debate into a constructive conversation where people work together toward transformation. What empowers empathetic listening for coaches is listening with curiosity. This means being curious about what qualities the other person possesses and trying to

THE TRANSCENDENCE LEADER-COACH (TLC)

see what can be learned. When leaders lean into coaching, they apply empathetic listening with curiosity and become genuinely interested in what their team has to contribute. They add value to a mutual learning journey. This amplifies the partnership between them. The more leaders act with a coach's curiosity, the more they ask, probe, and expand that learning capacity and horizon for the team. Therefore, that communication becomes a self-motivating relationship because it is based on reciprocity. Apart from creating that partnership, safe space, and empathetic mindset, coaching creates a culture of conversations. It is an empowerment vehicle that gives people the chance to open up, take charge, and contribute, leading to an inclusive environment.

The whole point of leaders embracing coaching is to embrace a human-centric approach. Coaching allows a deeper understanding of the human aspect behind the team members, making it fully human-centric i.e. understanding others as a whole and not only what they contribute to the organization.

TLCs believe that everyone has something to contribute. Everyone has a hidden gem that needs to be found, and the only way it can be found is to give the floor to others to come forward, open up, share their insights, and keep exploring their thoughts and deepening that learning so that they can expand their full capacity until they reach the desired level, that wavelength of creativity which will enable them to shine.

> *The reason why we say coaching is the highest level of communication is because of its embedded characteristics that enable objective observation and judgment-free conversations.*

2

THE VORTEX

Shifting Dynamics and Distortions

"Leadership is a way of thinking, a way of acting and, most importantly, a way of communicating."

— Simon Sinek[4]

Peter Senge coined the concept of dynamic complexity in his book *The Fifth Discipline: The Art & Practice of The Learning Organization*. He claims that the dynamic complexity that we are all engulfed in comes from the system's thinking: how we think, how we see things around us, and how we look at interconnecting parts within the system which has been even more amplified by the fast-tracked changes and developments taking place across the globe.[5]

But what truly adds to the dynamic complexity and makes it even more dynamic is human behavior. People are always evolving and have their values and emotions involved as they deal with challenges and interact with others. Most people are geared to think in a linear manner, whereas dealing with such dynamic complexity requires a nonlinear approach that allows leaders to embrace the human factor to start connecting to people rather than to challenges. When leaders look at people, they look at behavior, and when they look at behavior, they start looking at the behavioral change which is the most complex. To change the outcome, they need to change the actions or behaviors driving the outcome. This requires change in the actions and behaviors of people. It is complex as it means they have to disrupt existing habits (which manifest as automatic actions people have been used to doing for a long time) and embrace new behaviors which are possibly unfamiliar. The key here for the leaders is knowing how to support people to disrupt current behaviors, opening the door for new perspectives, and having an open mind to accepting what they are based on who they could be and not based on current manifested potential. It is all about expanding the thinking capacity of others, which is what coaching does.

> *"A good coach inspires his clients to envision their true potential, focus on what they can be rather than what they are now, empowering them to strive for greatness and transcend to new heights."*
>
> – IHAB BADAWI

This makes it important for leaders to focus on understanding human behavior more than operational matters. The more they go up the ladder of responsibility, the more their behavioral competencies need to be sharpened and the less they need to focus on operational competencies.

This is where the whole concept of coaching comes in. Coaching is at the heart of true leadership.

As I advocate coaching in organizations, the main thing I focus on is building a coaching culture or a culture of conversation within organizations. The only way to embrace that dynamic complexity and contribute toward that change within organizations is to have a leadership style or a leadership culture based on leadership-coaching, providing the chance for people to be listened to with trust and compassion, being able to lead and coach people from the heart, to connect with them by appreciating their diversity and including them in the process.

> Albert Einstein says, "The leader is the one who out of the clutter brings simplicity, out of discord, harmony, and out of difficulty, opportunity."

The Impact of the VUCA World

One of my favorite coaching experiences was witnessing one of my client's transformation while growing to become a global trader. The client was a sharp, goal-driven, and genuine CEO who took a trading business from a regional to a global level. In 15 years, the global economy shifted and technological advancements created a wave of developments that required internal transitions and adaptations.

Like most leaders at that time, the client's focus was mostly on the big game, on results, and on what was "out there" and not within the organization. Rapid changes in the technology serving the trade industry created volatile market dynamics and this created a blurry screen for the CEO making it hard to see internal requirements. Internal teams started feeling disengaged and not taken care of, yet this was not heard at the top. Uncertainty grew, and understanding causality to analyze and resolve market changes and consumer behavior became harder. Identifying the real causes was not straightforward anymore, which added to the pressure on this leader. The amount of data coming from global markets was ever-increasing, and the complexity of reports generated from 10 functions in 105 markets became a daily nightmare as days went by. Lack of decision-making and delayed actions started to affect every aspect of the organization, leading to inefficiencies and the erosion of profit margins.

With such a fragmented focus, this leader could not see through the growing ambiguity while, at the same time, insisting on taking the weight of the operation alone, believing that it was his duty to resolve major issues across the organization. This, by itself, led him to making the wrong decisions in savings, cutting the headcount in certain operations where the opposite was required. What was familiar became foreign even for such a successful and experienced leader.

During our coaching sessions, his belief in his own capacity to succeed and in the values of responsibility and ownership started showing a lack of understanding of the significance of adaptability and shared practice. It was not until that moment he realized that as external factors evolve and change, our practices, habits, and even our perspective of certain beliefs and values have to shift to maintain the balance. Growing the organization was no longer the only focus; it was what type of organization to grow and what culture to nurture from within, realizing that this was not the duty of the leader alone. He came to realize that the changes were not impacting him as a leader alone but impacting the team as well, who happen to have tremendous untapped potential.

A small shift in perspective caused by a coaching conversation opened this CEO's eyes and mind to see things from a fresh perspective. He understood that opening up to shared leadership comes from a point of power rather than weakness; that it is a step in trusting one's effort in building a team and trusting that team to be able to rise as future leaders. This shift in perspective led to the rise of shining stars within the organization. They proved they were capable of carrying part of the load and working as a team with the CEO to address the challenges. This was done by providing creative input to shape the strategy, driving smart saving plans, enhancing efficiency, and above all galvanizing the work environment, all leading to higher sales and increased profits in a happier working environment.

Leaders are surrounded by lots of changes creating noise around them. That noise creates clutter, a clutter that leaders and people, in general, have difficulty seeing through. It impacts the way leaders think, the way people connect, and the way they build a kind of foresight toward the future.

The rapid advances in technology have created a new environment that leaders are trying to continuously adapt to. The fast track of the internet and the development of smartphones bring a huge amount of information to their fingertips, which their brains are not geared to accommodate. Add to it the impact of the financial crisis that keeps returning, as in 2008, which increases the economic turbulence and unpredictability. Covid-19 and its impact on social interconnectedness, fast-tracked inflation and remote management, all adding to the pressures leaders have to deal with.

These changing dynamics are creating a huge burden that is shifting the usual operating platforms leaders were used to and adding to the noise around them. This has resulted in a kind of brain fog where people can't see as clearly as they used to; therefore, the era of forecasting five-year plans is completely over. They are lucky to be able to see one year ahead if they have a proper plan, and without a proper plan, the maximum they can see is the next six months. Still, it is impossible for them to see or predict what is coming, in terms of technology or in terms of the industries surrounding them, because they live in the VUCA world. They are unable to keep track of so many rapid changes. Many of those factors are beyond the capability of leaders who are still following the conventional leadership approach to try to withstand the change.

Volatility, Uncertainty, Complexity, Ambiguity

Volatility is the tendency to change rapidly and unpredictably for the worse. For leaders who want to look forward to dealing with that volatility, they realize that they need to alter their approach by trying to find a way to harness the internal factors while being able to withstand external ones. This can only happen when leaders face the fact that it is not them alone dealing with the VUCA world. Leaders should not be reacting to the next challenge that comes their way, but should rather be prepared to meet it when it arrives. The main tool that helps leaders prepare for change is adaptability, which will be discussed in upcoming chapters. If leaders are aware of and open to change, they can maintain control over change before pressures build to the point where action becomes futile.

Uncertainty is a state of being in doubt, where causes and effects are unknown. Uncertainty is dragging leaders to unpredictable future outcomes. They are uncertain of the results of whatever is being implemented. The impact is that the present is unclear; therefore, the future is uncertain. Hence, this adds to the pressure that leaders have to deal with. With uncertainty, they become hesitant and doubtful. This is usually felt across the whole organization and is the main cause leading to backfiring work upstream. Leaders should know that uncertainty is out of their hands and they cannot control it, which is why they should shift their attention to what they can control and eliminate. They should embrace uncertainty because it helps them understand their fears. When they learn to build a relationship with their fears, they build a relationship with the essence of themselves, and in every decision they make, subsists the opportunity for growth.

Complexity is fostered by the amount of and pace at which information is being consumed. Data is becoming huge with the evolution of technology and is being presented at a very high rate. Many leaders are having a hard time dealing with such data as they still believe it's their duty alone to process it. Dealing with human behavior here means dealing with dynamic complexity which is even harder. Leaders should identify the difference between what they can control and what they cannot and not mistake plans for reality. It is not about the product but about the process. Eisenhower claimed in his famous words "Plans are nothing, planning is everything." It is good to plan, but if opportunities and customers head in the other direction, the leader must embrace this sudden change and edit the plan as needed by engaging the team, and creating a thought-provocative process that reduces the complexity surrounding the organization.

Ambiguity is another factor that adds to the impact of the VUCA world. The environment being ambiguous adds to the lack of clarity or awareness about a certain situation. Ambiguity impacts leaders when they are unable to handle the many types of information they come across, resulting in them having a kind of fragmented awareness of the situation they are dealing with. As a result, leaders suffer from brain fog; consequently, they are unable to join the dots in whatever information they are receiving which causes them additional pressure. Leaders should stay focused and navigate through the chaos. They should prepare the organization ahead of time for any surprises by building a state of readiness at all times. Having flexible plans rather than fixed ones help the leader and the organization overcome any unforeseen obstacles, helping them to act calmly in the moment, rather than rejecting change and fighting in vain.

The VUCA impacts the whole organization, leading to organizational anxiety. Leaders have to understand that it is not their responsibility solely to tackle the VUCA world. It is a collective responsibility; and, leaders have to be the enablers.

The Impact of the VUCA World - Organizational Anxiety

Volatility, Uncertainty, Complexity, and Ambiguity destabilize people and make them anxious, and when they become anxious, pressure builds within the system. The impact of organizational anxiety can be felt in the:

1. *Lack of stability*: It eliminates people's motivation, or it sucks it out. People are impacted when they are not aware of what

awaits them the next day in relation to their work status. This impacts their sense of stability in their jobs and their ability to plan their career path or how their next move is going to look like.
2. *Difficulty retaining talent*: Anxiety within the organization builds pressure across all levels. It also builds pressure on the system within organizations which have a tough time maintaining or retaining existing talents. Planning becomes an issue not only for the leader but for the managers and supervisors, as losing talent leads to depleting the knowledge center.
3. *Delayed decision-making*: The impact of VUCA in some organizations creates paralysis in decision-making while trying to accommodate all the changes that take time to implement. Therefore, it creates a kind of holdup in moving forward which jeopardizes long-term projects and developments.

Accordingly, a different type of leadership that can support the team and the whole organization by embedding new characteristics, new competencies, and a new mindset is needed. The bottom line is, if not handled well or if leaders don't reshape the way they look at the VUCA world, the impact of the VUCA environment will create what is called an internal bleed within the system.

> *"Fatigue makes cowards of us all."*
>
> – Lombardi[6]

Anxiety brings about organizational fatigue. Fatigue leads leaders to amplify negatives rather than opportunities, create imagined problems, feel inadequate, block creativity, and tend towards blame. The impact is not only felt and reflected by others but it also trickles down through the whole organization.

"VUCA, a world of challenges yet full of opportunities for growth & innovation."

– IHAB BADAWI

Advocate Vitality vs Anxiety

The only way out of breaking the chains of anxiety, is by embracing vitality. The only way forward for leaders to create that change, is by implementing a kind of forward action and looking for what is positive and possible, and this is exactly what the essence of coaching is, facilitating the exploration of all what is positive and possible. People are driven with much more power when they are looking at where they are heading, and where they would like to reach. The internal potential of creativity, positivity, and hope are contagious: they trickle down and create a kind of positive energy across the organization.

"Leadership is irrelevant when results are guaranteed."

– NORMAN VINCENT PEALE

Vitality through a Coach's Mindset

True leaders shine when challenges arise. Certainty is inconceivable when problems are complex and multiple solutions could work. Therefore, leaders thrive when they face challenges, if they embrace a flexible mindset which is built on an agile way of thinking. Before they can be creative, they need to have that open mindset to enable them to notice opportunities and information that surrounds them. So, leaders should not wait for the perfect circumstances to fall into place since information is always incomplete and the results are seldom certain. Leaders should embrace vitality by adopting a new mindset that sets them on a course to constantly see what is possible for them while moving forward. By instilling a coach's mindset, leaders will be able to become curious about what's happening rather than being bogged down with details.

Embracing a coach's mindset enables leaders to be grounded, present in the moment, and capable of standing their ground while facing the winds. Having that sensibility and resilience enables leaders to look at the storm in slow motion rather than being swept away by it. They can step into the vortex unshaken, transcend slowly as they look at it, and calm that energy to see the components within that vortex, the components that will add value to them and their team.

THE VORTEX

TRANSCENDENCE
Coaching Model

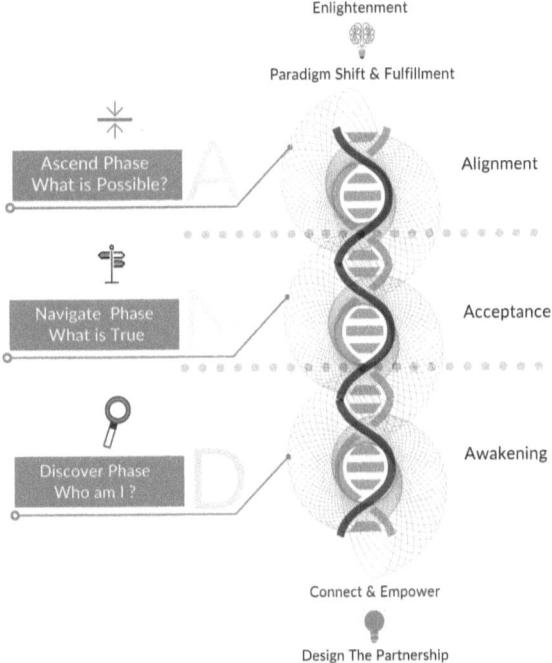

FIGURE 2.1: THE T- MODEL (THE TRANSCENDENCE MODEL OF COACHING) MANIFESTING TRANSCENDING AWARENESS WITHIN THE VORTEX

A key factor is that Leader-Coaches with that mindset are aware that it's not about them being able to transcend through the vortex alone. Leader-Coaches always remember that they are operating within a team, surrounded by the collective wisdom that they need to harness; therefore, they build on that partnership. Partnership can never be a one-way street; the

23

same goes for coaching. So, when Leader-Coaches embrace a coaching mindset, they are in partnership with all the people around them. They are courageous enough to step in and reach out to that team and include them in that process, and therefore evolve that leadership style so that it becomes more of an invitation for all those members to step in and contribute.

The big question now becomes: "Are they able to evolve their leadership style? Are they able to evolve to embrace the kind of leadership style that is required to face all these challenges in the future?"

> *"We can't solve problems by using the same kind of thinking we used when we created them."*
>
> – ALBERT EINSTEIN

In his book *What Got You Here Won't Get You There*, Marshall Goldsmith[7] summarizes a key message we are trying to share with all leaders. The message is that, whatever leadership approach has taken them so far will not take them any further. What they need is to evolve their leadership style and embrace a new set of competencies and a new mindset as leaders.

In the upcoming chapters, we will be covering the kind of mindset we, as leaders, need to have to evolve to become Transcendence Leader-Coaches. The kind of mindset pillars we need to embrace, and the kind of competencies to work on, shape, and build on so that we are able to become that Transcendence Leader-Coach who is able to face the VUCA world, avoid the anxiety, and surpass the aforementioned challenges.

3

THE PARADIGM SHIFT

"Leadership is not about being in charge. Leadership is about taking care of those in your charge."

— SIMON SINEK

What I like the most about the transformation journey of our esteemed CEO, part of whose journey I shared in the previous chapter, is the major shift of focus from external dynamics to internal ones. This is not to advocate for leaders not to look at the external industry or business indicators; but rather to shift focus toward what drives those dynamics internally, in order to shape the impact of external factors. Letting go of old leadership perspectives and embracing a more flexible and agile mindset unlocked the CEO's own creativity in dealing with others and facilitated innovation within the organization, not only in terms of business services but across business operations. He moved from being in charge and managing a team to building partnerships that developed a sense of trust, openness, and safety across the organization.

However, this was not the true gain. The true gain was in the creation of cross-functional bridges built on trust, and the rise of new talents who became more visible. What was really impressive was that the whole team gave credit to the CEO as they all understood that the continuous changes in the organization were leading to the development of a new organizational culture. The leader, the CEO, was embracing a step-by-step coaching approach with the team by becoming more of an observant listener, supporting the team to grow and expand their capacities, by providing the opportunity for healthy constructive conversations. His main aim was to eliminate obstacles and open the way for dynamic contributions from the teams.

As leaders realize that the old system is broken, they must now undergo a fundamental paradigm shift. Many leaders have used various smokescreens to cover their leadership approach with confidence and charisma while facing big challenges which, at some point, they have realized they couldn't overcome. They used to apply what they knew best; now they need to overcome those challenges by remembering that they are not living alone, that they are part of the organization, and believing that leadership is a complete chain, not a position. Leadership is a manifestation of what the whole team has contributed to the organization. This is where a major paradigm shift should occur among leaders. Their thought processes and belief systems should shift, as they migrate from a position of knowing everything and having all the answers, to asking for the team's contribution.

> *"Leaders should remember that they are not living alone, but are part of the organization, believing that leadership is a complete chain, not a position."*
>
> – IHAB BADAWI

Creativity and Innovation

As leaders witness the impact of the VUCA world and the various challenges that have been imposed on their teams, they must sense the need to maintain the level of creativity and innovation in an organization, which has become the most essential aspect of leadership. As a result, leaders have to invite people to improvise, contribute, and step up within the organization and toward the leader. This can only happen when leaders provide the opportunity for people to be engaged and included in the complete cycle within the organization, whether it is planning or implementation. Consequently, leaders have to change their existing system and embrace a completely different mindset. To provide the opportunity for people to be included, the first thing leaders have to do is become more flexible to allow various ideas and contributions to be delivered by the team. Leaders need to be flexible about accepting that concept first, and then start creating a culture of inclusion based on partnership.

Building Partnership

At the essence of coaching is building partnership with the client, or the coachee. The coach's main focus is on the person and not the issue at hand, be it a problem or an opportunity. By focusing on the "Who" of the person, the coach empowers a relationship based on TRUST. It is trust which empowers clients to open up and unlock their potential to find their own answers. By the same token, a leader-coach looks internally for opportunities to build shared partnerships rather than a one-way approach. The only way for leaders to harness the collective wisdom of the team is by reaching out and building partnerships through involvement. Part of showing trust, which is essential to build internal partnerships, is by involving the team and keeping them informed, and engaging them in discussions that open their mind. It is by focusing on the individuals within the team and their capacity to grow, that facilitates creative solutions rather than focusing on the problem itself.

Shared Leadership

Another manifestation of the new leadership is shared leadership. Shared leadership means that leaders understand that they should not always lead from the front. Often, they have to lead from the sides or the back. They must delegate as much as they can and place other people in the forefront to breed new leaders, as part of a consistent dynamic operation of evolving the team to assume new leadership roles. This means that true authentic leaders must go beyond the concept of delegation, and more into the concept of complete empowerment, looking at building a leadership model based on collective leadership through all team members. To accomplish this, they need to start accepting the unknown and having the courage to step into it. This way, leaders will be able to transform and move from the "I know" position to embracing the unknown. By transcending to a leader-coach, leaders become grounded, and more geared to explore the unknown without anticipating the answers. Coaching is a quest and exploration of what is possible without adopting any agenda by the coach. It is by being completely objective, and judgment-free that the coach is able to invite the coachee to explore the unknown safely. The coach and the coachee explore safely based on partnership and both become leaders on the way. This is shared leadership.

Accepting the Unknown

A major part of Leader-Coaches' mindset is accepting the unknown and accepting that every challenge or opportunity is a chance for exploration. To lean into the unknown means accepting vulnerability and agreeing with enough courage to go to a place where not all answers are available. So, for leaders to be able to operate with their teams, they must embrace that coaching mentality of looking at everything through the lens of exploration.

"To lead is to serve."

– Francis of Assisi

Serving Others

Evolving to an even higher level is the service mindset, whereby leaders are no longer reaching out to find a solution for them to act upon but are looking to delegate and empower the team and follow this up with one question: "How can I serve you?" In doing so, leaders embrace that service mentality in facilitating the way for their team to shine as leaders. The focus of leaders at that point becomes eliminating obstacles, eliminating any kind of roadblock that might prevent or delay the team from moving forward. The biggest contributor to a service mindset is coaching itself.

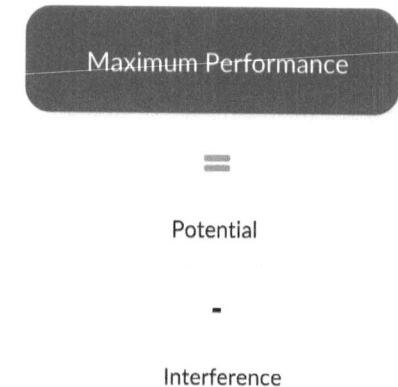

FIGURE 3.1: BEING OF SERVICE FOSTERS A SENSE OF CONNECTION AND EMPATHY. CONNECTING WITH OTHERS CREATES A SPACE OF TRUST, MUTUAL RESPECT, AND OPEN COMMUNICATION.

Interference, in this formula, is any obstacle that might stand in the way of any individual thus reducing the maximum performance based on their true potential. By enabling the team to identify interferences and finding ways to eliminate them, Leader-Coaches maximize the team's performance exponentially, first by eliminating obstacles so their performance is realized based on their true potential, and then by stretching their capacity to maximize their potential. The fastest way leaders can maximize the performance of their team is to eliminate interference. This allows the team to operate on the existing potential with no drawbacks. Eliminating the barriers for the team fosters trust, and empowers the partnership even further, opening doors for the leader-coach to explore the hidden potential of the team, thus compounding the effect of maximizing their performance.

> *Being of Service fosters a sense of connection & empathy. Connecting with others creates a space for trust, mutual respect & open communication.*

4

EMBRACING THE COACHING APPROACH

*"Integrity, insight, and inclusiveness are
the three essential qualities of leadership."*

— *Sadhguru*[8]

I will never forget an inspiring lesson I learnt from someone I am proud to have had within my team. We acquired an organization in Africa which had been suffering for five years from not being able to increase revenues. I was leading the business operations team at that time with a mandate to develop the region. Apart from building the nucleus of the new team from within, we lacked few talents and it was challenging to integrate new team members into leadership positions as we had to factor in cultural gaps. One of my main priorities was to bring in leaders who shared the values we were trying to instill as part of the internal transition, and not to fall into the negative work environment that was dominant in that entity due to bad practices from earlier leaders.

One of the main factors which made me decide to recruit that team member was based on his sense of integrity, and not just his technical expertise. To this day I am proud of such a decision. It was his integrity that guided his leadership style to build an operation based on transparency. In turn, his leadership style led to strong team engagement and a safe working environment where the highs and lows were shared with no fear of possible consequences, based on a sense of ownership without jeopardizing accountability. Working closely to build a new operation and having a shared set of values, we were able to transform the operation and increase its revenue nine-fold in only eleven months. The sense of pride walking into this operation and sensing the spirit of belonging, trust, and positivity was beyond my imagination. Full credit should go to this new leader who was aligned with the core values we intended to instill. It was his own leadership style and care that enabled the transformation. And if a process was to take credit, it would be coaching. Instilling a coaching culture from day one of taking over, and using this entity as a testing ground to expand to other operations was a great decision. People felt important after being listened to. They could contribute and be taken seriously. Their ideas were displayed on the walls and used to discuss and explore new input. Everybody became hungry to contribute, learn, and grow. Empathetic listening and curious inquiry, with complete presence to witness what would come, was the name of the game.

What empowers leadership is the ability to be honest and authentic, not only in the way leaders conduct business but in the way they approach their team. Having an authentic approach cultivates a culture of integrity across the organization, ensuring that as leaders they have the capability to create insight for the team. This means that they are contributing to raising the team's awareness to have a better perspective on matters. The greater the empowerment of the team through heightened awareness and visibility, the more empowered the organization will be.

Team Engagement

One of the important indicators of organizational health and power of leaders is measuring the engagement level of employees. Engagement is much higher than job satisfaction. Engagement means that employees are involved in the operation, know and understand where the organization is heading, understand the vision, and have contributed to the shared vision that they believe in. They understand what their role is, what their added value is, and what they are capable of contributing to that relationship. For this to manifest itself in the organization, leaders have to resist the temptation to give all the answers and all the advice. They have to allow others the freedom to come up with their own solutions and ideas. They can act as facilitators for the creative new thinking process, but they should refrain from stepping into that process and provide answers. This is where coaching becomes an empowerment tool for leaders because coaching disciplines leaders to self-manage and to hold back from stepping in and giving advice. Instead, they listen objectively to what others have to contribute. Coaches never give answers or advice even when they have the answer. Their focus is on expanding others' capacity by expanding the way they think. Coaching provides a tangible way for leaders to show that they believe in growth and in the success of other people, which eventually builds trust. Trust is a key accelerator for engagement and creativity. It is the key to establishing a safe environment where failure is acceptable and making mistakes is tolerated as a means of learning.

Safe Accountability

When leaders offer advice and team members follow this advice, leaders become fully responsible for the outcome. Leaders need to take responsibility, but they should not deprive other people of being responsible or accountable for their contributions because when leaders give directions and it fails, the first thing that the team will do is point fingers at leaders which creates a blame culture. However, if leaders want to create a more engaging culture that fosters new leaders, they should allow the chance for people to come up with their own solutions and take ownership. If their solution turns out to be a success, they are rewarded, recognized, and celebrated across the whole organization. Should their solutions not work, leader-coaches would enable them the space to reflect and see it as a learning opportunity, rather than failure, empowering them to hold themselves accountable rather than fear the consequences. By coaching the team to step out of the failure mentality, leaders can maximize the potential of their team and create a safe space for self-accountability. Imagine how much time and effort is saved for leaders by implementing this approach!

Bridging Fear

While listening objectively and with no judgment, coaching facilitates an invitation for conversations without fear. Most people don't like conflict, and they don't like the fear that is attached to it. When coaches engage clients or team members in a coaching process by being listeners, by acting as sounding boards, without trying to analyze or provide solutions, they are inviting people to bridge their fear. This is done by providing a safe space for them to open up and talk about their concerns, challenges, or even the opportunities awaiting them. Fear diminishes when people have the chance to talk, the conversation creates new neural pathways in their brains which allows them to connect their rational brain with their subconscious. Their subconscious holds great power that will support them in finding new ways to move forward, and this helps them build more confidence. Coaching supports people to find that hidden inner potential: it supports people to tap into their subconscious to find all those stored capabilities, capacities, and information and apply them to whatever is on the table, so that they become more creative and see things from a different perspective.

This is why coaches operate from a space that considers every person as naturally creative, resourceful, and whole. By believing so, coaches are starting from a positive space that is based on trusting that clients are capable of finding their own solutions. So, by allowing people to talk more, open up, share, and contribute, their creativity is evoked. The idea is to build on that creativity by inviting people to stand up and take a step forward. In doing so, people have to feel that they have control or authority over the situation.

Being in the NOW Moment

The TLCs are leaders who lead without authority or position. They need no authority to connect themselves with the state of being: they are connected to the NOW moment, to the team members, and to the organization and society. This ensures that leaders can transcend the materialistic connection to a position and lead others without the authoritative behavior. To do so, leaders need to master self-awareness and control through Emotional Resilience.

Practicing Emotional Resilience

To be in a state of being, leaders have to master emotional resilience, which is being able to calm the thought processes after encountering a negative experience. Emotional resilience, simply put, is the capacity of leaders to bounce back from adversity. The capacity to build emotional resilience includes the capacity to build self-acceptance, devise stress management strategies, build self-esteem, be mindful and focused on the present expression, express emotions wisely, and choose to react to stress in a way that won't harm themselves or others.

> *Nelson Mandela once said, "The greatest glory and living lies not in falling, but in rising every time we fall."*[9]

Leading from that mindset frees leaders from any fear of failure, because having the belief that they can rebound provides them the courage to explore unknown areas. Leaders can empower their team with the same approach by providing them with the confidence to believe in themselves.

What supports leaders to become more resilient is:

1. Being aware of thoughts, emotions, and inner potential.
2. Thinking before reacting; counting to ten, letting things resonate, and looking at things objectively rather than emotionally. It is said that it takes six seconds for the

logical mind (neocortex) to counteract the emotional mind (amygdala).
3. Being patient, understanding, and willing to adapt.
4. Being high on acceptance: accepting what is and what is coming, leaning more into forgiveness, focusing on finding solutions, and focusing on positivity and hope.
5. Prioritizing health which means taking care of the mind, body, and spirit. Leader-Coaches ensure their own wellbeing in order to provide that wellbeing for others.
6. Finding support which means communicating, cooperating, reaching out, surpassing conflicts rather than just avoiding them, working with mindfulness, focusing on one task at a time, and creating a focus that will open doors to being in a state of flow that allows people to be deeply engaged in the task at hand.
7. Applying the capacity to listen with appreciation and acceptance rather than judging. This will facilitate an objective understanding of the surrounding environment.

The Magic of Presence

> *"When there is lack of leadership presence, people feel unheard and frustrated."*
>
> – IHAB BADAWI

If leaders can manifest the presence of coaches by being connected to the now moment, anyone who encounters those

EMBRACING THE COACHING APPROACH

leaders feels their presence and is motivated to open up. Opening up has a positive effect on the chemistry of human brains. It cultivates human's capacity to access a higher thought process that gives access to the wisdom that comes from heightened awareness, the compassion that comes from increased openness, and the confidence that comes from the strength of allowing the person to be aligned from within. In practice, presence has a huge impact on people. Being able to connect to the NOW is inspiring as it allows people to start noticing what they have missed. Leaders who are capable of manifesting a coach's presence are comfortable, humble, and engaged at all times. They are friendly and approachable. They speak with conviction, clarity, and respect.

The bottom line, leadership presence is the capability to connect authentically, build confidence, and inspire and motivate others to take action, which gives them the power to innovate and become more engaged. When leaders embrace the coach's presence, they unlock the power to focus on the capability to gain power over the brain and heart, to direct their attention to what is most important, and therefore to go beyond the existing filters. Once focused, leaders will be able to see much more clearly. They become empowered as they will have the capacity to eliminate distractions that act as obstacles to them and the team. With such focus, that comes from presence, leaders can act like coaches by connecting with themselves to tap into their inner potential, and be in control of raising that potential when needed, sharing it with those around them.

5

THE CONSCIOUS LEADER-COACH

Leading from Multi-Dimensional Awareness

"Multidimensional problems require multidimensional thinking. To find simple, actionable, single-task solutions, we need multidimensional thinkers to strike at the heart of things."

– RICHIE NORTON[10]

The Transcendence Leader-Coach is someone who leads neither through authority nor through position. The TLC is capable of transcending the materialistic barriers of geography and hierarchy, which usually confine a leader to a position, and is able to connect with the whole team as individuals rather than positions. The TLC is neither attached to title nor position, but rather to a state of "being." Another synonym for the TLC would be the conscious leader who leads from a place of full consciousness and heightened awareness.

What Is Conscious Leadership?

Early on in my career, as I look back at my conversations with my coach and mentor, I realize his questions were never about the leaders I used to complain about. The questions were all about the type of leader I wanted to be, my vision, and the values I was willing to embrace and defend at all costs. One of the things he once said, "If you want to lead, lead through intention, set your course right, and have a destination as to what type of person you want to be, not only for you but for those who matter to you. Let the intention sink in and then let the power of intention drive you, and have an intention that bares no doubt. Lead yourself first, based on those values, before you lead others. When you do so you will not have to put in the effort to lead others. You will lead them by inspiration. Just remain true to what you stand for and be clear as to what your priorities are. Be confident while being conscious as to where you stand within your surrounding and always push to be better. Not better than others but better than the best version of you a moment ago."

> *"Conscious leaders focus on the culture of "WE" rather than "I." Guided by their intuition & connecting with the human within."*
>
> – Ihab Badawi

His words opened my eyes toward consciousness, to be conscious of myself and my surroundings, and to focus on those who matter the most: family and team. Having spent the first part of my experience in the Middle East, I started embracing the value of family in relation to a team; leading the team as a family by trusting and serving it while maintaining the grip of what is keeping the bond together, a shared vision of how that family would look in the future. I became conscious of myself, and being part of a group allowed my consciousness to rise, to start noticing and appreciating the virtues of each individual, and being intentional in listening, appreciating, and engaging to learn more, therefore fueling my curiosity to learn.

Even my language transformed, moving to the "WE" rather than the "I." It was about developing a collective consciousness rather than an individual one that led to a multi-dimensional awareness. This awareness opened the potential for laser focus and high attention. In seven years of this transformation, I was able to become the head of a half-billion-dollar operation, which the team and I later took to the billion-dollar benchmark.

In short, conscious leadership is the process by which a leader becomes radically responsible for being self-aware and focusing on the culture of "WE" rather than "I." Conscious leadership operates on the interconnectedness of leaders and their surroundings, including the team and the environment. It is about creating unity based on connection, the creation of relationships, and belief in one another. It allows leaders to be guided by their intuition, to be free from following only their logic and analytical skills, and to connect with the human within, who is capable of seeing other people and their capabilities.

Embracing conscious leadership enables leaders to experience an awakening that allows them to connect with their surroundings for the greater good of the group or the organization, rather than looking at their own goals and achievements. By embracing conscious leadership, the TLCs are conscious that achievement is at its highest when it takes into consideration everyone else in the formula. The goal of conscious leaders is to recognize how they might be reacting, thinking, and leading before taking any steps. So, conscious leaders are aware of everything happening within and everything surrounding them and are able to connect the dots so that they can understand the kind of impact their leadership style, or actions have on the team and the organizational environment, and society as a whole. To embrace that consciousness, leaders have to embrace certain commitments in order to manifest that kind of leadership in everything they do.

Commitment one: Taking radical responsibility. Not only in relation to the position or the goals at hand, but also for the team involved, for the people who are connected, and for all stakeholders and everyone involved in the process.

Commitment two: Being curious. By embracing conscious leadership, leaders need to commit to continuous learning based on curiosity. Curiosity drives interest, creativity, and growth by encouraging leaders to always be inquisitive, looking at every opportunity or challenge as a space to learn something new and to learn about the people involved.

Commitment three: Showing appreciation. The commitment to show and reflect appreciation to others and to whatever has been offered to them, anchors such leadership, because people will feel valued, trusted, and appreciated, and will therefore be motivated to give more, share more, and support more.

By embracing conscious leadership, leaders commit to opening up, embracing compassion, and having the capability to connect with others and understand what they are going through. This will help leaders appreciate where they are coming from and, therefore, take it into consideration. This is where leaders embrace a more humane approach to leadership by committing to integrity and honesty so that they speak candidly when voicing opinions or sharing feedback. An important aspect of TLCs is their capability to communicate at a high level, in a clear, candid, and safe manner that allows people to accept such feedback. And since they lean into what's positive and possible, like coaches, then they provide feed-forward, thus leveraging insights and potential while acting with the focus on the goal and discussions about how to recap what was lost, rather than spending time on past events or mistakes.

To embrace conscious leadership, leaders need to lead themselves before leading others.

Lead Oneself First

> *"A leader's wholeness lies in the intersection between his genius, purpose, passion, and excellence."*
>
> – Anonymous

An internal alignment is found at the intersection of the IQ, which reflects mental capability; the EQ, which is emotional intelligence and awareness; and the BQ, which is related to behavioral intelligence and how it affects the whole being of the person. Most leaders used to focus on the power of the IQ, decision-making, critical thinking, and strategic thinking, but not on leading self, emotional intelligence, and behavioral intelligence. The most important factor that transcends the Leader-Coaches is mastering that elevated self-knowledge and consciousness about where they stand, enabling them to harness the power of their internal intuition, and therefore guide their intelligence on a more informed ground about themselves.

> *"To be conscious leaders requires that we speak with integrity and lead with authenticity."*
>
> – Anonymous

Ego Check

Conscious leaders are in tune with themselves internally and with their surroundings. Therefore, they lean more into active listening and processing what is being listened to with patience and curiosity. The main aspect of conscious leaders that differentiates the TLCs from others is the ability to keep their egos in check, especially when interacting with others. Keeping the ego in check enables objective and empathetic listening. It enables listening without filters, without the need to be right which empowers the communication between the leaders and the team. Leaders listen to understand, rather than to convince. And listen to appreciate, rather than to criticize or blame. This is the first step of opening up to the team.

Intention

Most leaders focus on how to create an impact on others. Impact and influence are categorized under what is called the outer game which is driven by action. TLCs embrace the inner game first. They look inwards at their own mindset and how it affects them, and later look at its influence on other people. TLCs try to master the inner game by intention. Having an intention means having a drive, having a focus, and being driven by a vision of themselves and where they want to be, which acts as their true "why," their "true North." That sense of drive or the intention to be at a particular point in the future supersedes any kind of action. Having clarity on that vision drives them internally and provides them with the motivation to move forward. That motivation is amplified by the TLCs' capacity to be self-aware of their emotions, knowing where they want to be, what they value, what belief system they adopt, what their frame of reference is, and how they affect their perspective and decision-making process. Another element that supports the inner game is developing balanced self-confidence rather than being arrogant or overly confident.

Balanced Confidence

Confidence comes from leaders knowing that they have the necessary capacity and strength, and knowing to what level they can be stretched. This self-confidence alone drives their curiosity toward growth, for themselves and others. This self-confidence provides a positive outlook toward themselves and others by eliminating negative self-judgment and the possibility of disregarding others' capabilities.

Self-Efficacy

The last point TLCs focus on while mastering the inner game is self-efficacy, which is the belief that whatever comes their way can be handled. This makes them open to listening to feedback, accepting it, working on themselves based on that feedback, and then taking action. Having that self-efficacy coupled with confidence enables the TLCs to engage with others, have the courage to ask questions, connect with them, and elicit feedback from them. This becomes a continuous journey of self-development because the TLCs realize that being in that partnership requires constantly checking-in with others on what's transpiring and evolving, what kind of impact is being created around them, and how it is impacting them.

> *"When the Transcendence Leader-Coach embraces conscious leadership and is able to master the inner game, the outer game becomes a natural outcome to be mastered."*
>
> – IHAB BADAWI

Multi-Dimensional Awareness

Leaders are able to embrace a multi-dimensional awareness by being aware of themselves, their physical aspect, and how they manifest their leadership presence by the way they walk, communicate, and pay attention to minute details without effort. When they are in a state of being, they are able to command their leadership presence in front of others and reflect the best image with full authenticity and without makeovers through having awareness at multiple levels: physical, imaginative, emotional, and mental.

Physical

Having physical awareness is being aware of all the elements in their physical environment, all the factors surrounding them, the team, and the organization. This involves being conscious of the working environment and the work culture stemming from people's behavior and the organizational systems affecting it. Before commanding behavioral change, leaders need to examine the factors impacting the behavior and understand that the behavior is a reaction and not an action. Otherwise, all efforts to change behaviors will be reversed at one point as the physical factors have not been attended to. This includes not just the physical space, but also factors such as lighting, temperature, noise levels, and even air quality. For example, a poorly lit workspace can lead to eye strain, headaches, and decreased productivity, while excessive noise levels can cause stress and distractions. Leaders who prioritize physical awareness will take steps to ensure that their team's physical environment supports their well-being and enhances their ability to perform their job. This may involve making small adjustments, such as providing ergonomic chairs or adjusting the lighting, or larger changes, such as redesigning the layout of the workspace. By paying attention to the physical elements of the work environment, leaders can create a more supportive and productive workplace for their team.

Imaginative

Having imaginative awareness is being aware of insights, dreams and creative thoughts. The TLCs are able to crystallize that imagination and articulate it to themselves and those around them. They are able to take command of that imaginative process so that they become more intentional about what to create and how to explore those ideas to make them more tangible and translate them into the bottom line. Imaginative awareness is the ability to think creatively and outside of the box. This involves not only seeing what is in front of you but also the possibilities that exist beyond that. Leaders with imaginative awareness can envision new solutions to old problems, inspire others to think outside of their comfort zones, and take calculated risks to achieve success. This type of awareness requires an open mind and a willingness to explore new ideas and perspectives. Leaders who cultivate imaginative awareness can bring about positive change in their organizations by encouraging innovation, adaptability, and flexibility. By embracing the power of imagination, leaders can push their teams to new heights and achieve remarkable results.

Emotional

Having emotional awareness is being able to understand one's emotions as they arise in the moment, being able to detach from those feelings, noticing what triggers them, and identify the energy that is driving them. TLCs have a better command of self-management, which enhances their leadership presence, as they manage their emotions, resulting in more influence and a better capability to inspire others through intentional action, rather than an impulsive emotional response. Emotional responses come from a state of clouded judgment and impulse, and therefore may often be rushed and regretted. TLCs are well aware of what's happening in the moment and therefore are more in control of their reactions.

Mental

Having mental awareness is being mindful of the thought processes. The TLCs are able to transcend thought processes and understand how they are formulated and the kind of frame of reference that is driving them. This drives the TLCs' empathy and capability to understand how their thought processes are built and start appreciating them. In addition, they start understanding how other people's thought processes are built and where they are coming from without judgment or subjectivity.

> *"People are attracted to the sense of fairness as it makes them feel less anxious and safer."*
>
> – IHAB BADAWI

Facilitate Dialogue: Conscious Conversations

TLCs are able to understand their own perceptions, how they are formed, and how they can expand into different perspectives which strengthen their decision-making capacity and ability to connect with others. From this, the TLCs are able to facilitate dialogue with others that enables them to see things from a different perspective while they practice empathetic listening (as mentioned earlier in Chapter 1). Various studies have reflected that the quality of a culture in a country or an organization reflects the quality of the conversations that people have within that organization. In an article published in the Harvard Business Review, Judith E. Glaser argues that the quality of conversations within an organization can have a significant impact on its culture. She suggests that conversations that are "fear-based" or "power-based" can create a culture of mistrust and defensiveness, while conversations that are "trust-based" and "relationship-based" can create a culture of openness and collaboration. (Glaser, J. E. (2013). The secret to changing organizational culture.)

> *"Monitor the way people talk in company hallways and meetings, listen to the quality of their conversations, it will give you an indication of their beliefs and behaviors that shape and cultivate the organizational culture."*
>
> – IHAB BADAWI

Many studies have proven that the effectiveness of an organization, measured by the key business factors of growth, innovation, customer excellence, and efficiency, is driven by the way people act and behave, which ultimately drives the results. The way people behave and interact reflects how they communicate. The quality of their communication is driven by the level of conversations they have. The level of conversation is affected by the level of awareness that leaders instill in the organization. Conscious leadership is about creating conscious conversations that are directed at understanding the external and internal systems, and are designed to shape the intended new reality. If they don't have open, honest, and objective conversations free from judgment, they will end up failing to share information and lacking trust and openness. Organizational operations will slow down because things will take time to develop when information is withheld. Time and effort are being wasted in resolving conflicts due to judgments that will hinder efficiency and the growth cycle within the organization. In the absence of conscious conversations, people start holding back as a result of not feeling safe to speak the truth, and they become discouraged from opening up. They will end up caring less.

> *"Silence becomes a silent killer of the motivation and the morale of the organization."*
>
> — IHAB BADAWI

Organizations that embrace open communication based on trust, integrity, and belief in one another, report higher levels of team functioning, employee engagement, and productivity, improved employee relations, and greater internal leadership development, all of which ensure the sustainability and continuity of the organization. Therefore, embracing coaching at a leadership level fosters that resilient leadership type. By becoming TLCs, leaders are able to lead in the moment, and lead from within. Leading from within means from a space of trust and courage, integrity, openness, and connection free of judgment and personalization which ensures that the culture can thrive and create new leaders through conscious conversations.

Reflective Questions: For Multi-Dimensional Awareness

Voltaire once wrote, "Judge a man by his questions rather than by his answers."[11]

- ❖ How comfortable am I talking about my feelings, and with whom?
- ❖ What upsets me about other people's behavior, and what does that say about me?
- ❖ How do I handle difficult but necessary conversations?
- ❖ What positive qualities do I bring into my close relationships?
- ❖ In what ways am I contributing to my family, organization or community?
- ❖ What activities make me feel content, energized, and fulfilled?
- ❖ What are my strategies for bouncing back after a failure?

- How would I describe myself in one sentence?
- What limiting beliefs do I hold about myself and the world?
- What compliment do I like to hear the most and why?
- What challenges have I faced in the past that I'm proud of overcoming?
- What mistake did I learn the most from?
- When was the last time I said "NO" and felt good about it?
- What one thing would I do if my success was guaranteed?
- If I could offer advice to my teenage self, what would I say?
- What would I do differently if I knew nobody would judge me?
- Am I on the right path in life? How can I tell?
- What accomplishments am I most proud of?
- What changes have I undergone that I thought impossible five years ago?
- When was the last time I felt empowered?
- What is the best decision I've ever made?

Enhancing Multi-Dimensional Awareness

Reflect on your actions and write down in each category 3 actions that will drive you closer to the best version of yourself as a Transcendence Leader-Coach.

KEEP DOING	START DOING	STOP DOING

SECTION II

In today's fast-paced and ever-changing business environment, the role of a leader coach has become more critical than ever. To be an effective leader coach, one must embrace a unique mindset, the TLC's mindset which is built on 6 main pillars: **abundance**, **bliss**, **positivity**, **forward-thinking**, **growth**, and **gratitude**. This mindset serves as a foundation for building a resilient and agile approach to leadership, allowing leaders to shift their reality and adapt to changing circumstances. This mindset encourages leaders to focus on what they can achieve rather than what they lack or what could go wrong. As a result, they are better able to inspire and motivate their teams to achieve great things together.

Leaders need to embrace a new way of thinking that emphasizes collaboration, communication, and connection. In this context, the leader-coach mindset is becoming increasingly essential for leaders who want to achieve exceptional results, while building a culture of growth and development.

Moreover, to be successful, Leader-Coaches must also develop a set of competencies that enable them to create deep connections with their team, demonstrate versatility in their leadership style, and deliver authentic service. Finally, trust is paramount, as it forms the foundation of all successful relationships. Therefore, in the following chapters, we will explore in-depth how leaders can develop the Transcendence Leader-Coach mindset, create connection, develop versatility, and build authentic service while fostering trust in their team and organization.

The six pillars of the Transcendence Leader-Coach mindset will pave the way for leaders to manifest sixteen competencies essential for each leader. I have grouped the sixteen core competencies, which I have discovered during my research to be powerful in shaping the leader's approach especially when manifested together. I believe every TLC needs to have these competencies. They are grouped into four clusters. Cluster one is **Connection**, two is **Versatility**, three is **Service**, and four is **Trust**. Each cluster is made up of four competencies that work together. By combining the four clusters, we will witness the interconnection between the sixteen competencies which are at the core of the TLC's behavior.

In the following chapters, we will explore the six pillars of the TLC mindset which prepare the ground for leaders to understand and accept, and therefore implement, all of these core competencies. Just as values act as the platform of behavior, these competencies act as the platform of the TLC's behavior; and the competencies are grouped in four clusters: **Connection**, how leaders can create connection within their teams, building a sense of community and belonging that drives engagement and productivity; **Versatility**, exploring how leaders can adapt their leadership style to meet the needs of different team members and situations; **Service**, which emphasizes the importance of putting others first and building trust through empathy and active listening; and finally **Trust** as the key to open and authentic conversations, exploring how leaders can build trust with their teams and create a culture of transparency and honesty.

6

THE TRANSCENDENCE LEADER-COACH MINDSET

Building a Resilient Mindset to Shift Reality

There are various competencies that coaches manifest to be able to support clients in undergoing a transformative experience. These competencies rely on a solid base which is the coach's mindset. Without the right mindset, coaches will not be able to embrace the wholeness of the self and that of the clients. There are six interconnected pillars that shape the coaches' presence and connection with the clients and reflect on the clients themselves. This mindset is contagious and clients start resembling those six pillars throughout an effective session. These are the same six pillars that leaders can embrace to establish new connections with their team.

FIGURE 6.1: THE 6 PILLARS OF THE TLC MINDSET

"Clients are naturally creative, resourceful, and whole."

— ICF PRINCIPLE

This is the motto of all professional coaches. Coaches believe in the capacity of the clients to have the inner creativity to come up with their own answers or ways of moving forward. If for some reason their creativity is not tapped, clients can tap into their resourcefulness to reach out to find the answers. Coaches believe that clients are whole systems within systems. Therefore, coaches support clients to dive deep to find the inner systems that will enable them to identify the external systems they can reach out for support.

This belief cannot be maintained without the six main pillars of the coach's mindset. To have that belief, coaches have to embrace gratitude by being grateful for the opportunity to influence others. Gratitude fosters blissful thinking, a joyful positive curiosity, and the hope that the clients will find their own answers. Coaching is all about what is positive and possible. The possibility comes from the belief in abundance and multiplicity, the fact that there are many perspectives we can look at that will change the world around us. With such a world of opportunities, coaches fuel the clients' belief that growth can occur every second of the session, and with growth comes forward thinking: the capacity to have an eye on the future rather than looking backward. This is why coaching is about the now moment: what is decided now shapes the future; hence, the focus is on what is positive and possible rather than on the past and the negative.

> *"Many focus on actions while forgetting that it all starts with the mindset."*
>
> – Ihab Badawi

With the same token, mindset is what drives the leadership style, what drives leaders to be intentional about the type of leadership they want to show in an organization or society. The main challenge for all managers on their path toward leadership and all leaders on their path toward becoming TLCs is how much they are capable of shifting from the old mentality of always being in the pilot's seat to accepting the new position of sitting in the co-pilot's seat. It's about embracing a mindset that is open and flexible, that accepts evolution and adaptation as part of an automatic progression. This means adapting to current circumstances while having an eye on the future: adapting to changes while preparing for future evolution.

Albert Einstein said, "We cannot resolve problems with the same mindset that created them." Leaders can't face the complexities of the VUCA world with the same mindset they usually employ. It requires a new mindset to turn adversities into opportunities. Negativity yields skepticism, which holds any leader back from trying a new path. It impacts the whole organization and halts its efforts. Looking at things through a lens of scarcity, limits the vision of any leader and pushes toward a reductive rather than an expansive approach. This leads to limitations and backward movement. It requires a completely new thought basis that fosters creativity and innovation.

> *The main challenge for all managers on their path toward leadership and all leaders on their path toward becoming TLCs is how much they are capable of shifting from the old mentality of always being in the pilot's seat to accepting the new position of sitting in the co-pilot's seat.*

"Leaders cannot create what they lack. They can't expect from others what they can't expect from themselves."

– Ihab Badawi

Toxic Environments

Leaders have to be aware of toxic environments that are based on negative emotions within the work environment as they create barriers to growth.

Envy: Negative emotions yield envy, and envy between team members will travel fast within the organization. Envy is unhealthy for the growth environment. Actually, it limits it. Envy is based on the belief that if I don't have it no one should. This is a limiting thinking process that does not facilitate growth as a team.

Self-Pity: Another negative emotion that yields negativity is self-pity which puts people in a discounting mindset. Leaders start discounting their capability and looking at what they have lost and lose the capacity to look at what they can gain. As a result, opportunities pass them without noticing. With time, self-pity creates bitterness which turns people harder toward each other and themselves. Therefore, interpersonal and interfunctional relationships within an organization become slower due to inflexibility which is a result of bitterness.

Entitlement: Entitlement is another feature that is linked to negative emotions. Entitlement is when leaders feel that the organization owes them, that their colleagues owe them, and their relationships are built around a sense of: "I need more, just because this is who I am. I'm special, and what I do is special." Entitlement does not appreciate what others do. And the lack of appreciation leads to reduced engagement and, eventually, to a complete disengagement from the organization.

Negative emotions in general tend to be destructive to the work environment and weaken bonds within the team. Without those bonds, the whole body of the organization becomes weaker. To fortify the organization and the team, the leaders' main duty is to spread positivity across the organization at each touchpoint. To do this, leaders need to do it effortlessly. That means leaders should be convinced of the power of positivity, and therefore, have positivity as an anchor or a main pillar within the Leader-Coach mindset.

So, what is it that leaders need as a mindset?

Negative emotions, fostering envy, self-pity, entitlement, fear, low self-esteem, and negative emotions are a result of what goes on in the mental processes. They are all a result of what people prime their minds with, which moves from the frontal cortex, the logical or conscious brain, into the subconscious which is the most powerful part of the brain. The thoughts fed to the brain define what people start believing and eventually feeling and acting on.

Studying leaders across 58 countries, I found that all top leaders have certain empowering beliefs in common that served to differentiate them from others. I say beliefs, and not behaviors because it started with them believing in a set of values and priming their subconscious to manifest them as behaviors, that later shaped their character. Accordingly, I have grouped those empowering beliefs under six pillars that shape the TLC Mindset.

The Six Pillars of a TLC's Mindset

The six pillars of a Transcendence Leader-Coach's mindset are gratitude, bliss, abundance, positivity, growth, and forward-thinking.

As we look at each pillar, we will start to uncover how each can help in creating the mindset of the TLC to face the fast-paced changes and the dynamic complexity that surrounds us. The TLCs will be able to face volatility, uncertainty, complexity, and ambiguity through the power of being grounded and connected. They will succeed with a vision that will allow them to cut through the chaos, above all connect to others, and harness the collective wisdom and the power of the group.

1. Gratitude: Gratitude is what allows the TLCs to act from a state of acceptance and fulfillment, a state of accepting the current reality, accepting what's happening, while having an objective realization of all the surrounding elements, changes, and challenges. At the same time, their acceptance must be driven by a sense of fulfillment throughout their journey, and not only when they reach their destination or when the goals are achieved. As a result, they can reflect this gratitude to their environment and those around them, because:

> *"Fulfillment for the Transcendence Leader-Coach is not a destination but rather a state."*
>
> – Ihab Badawi

Fulfillment is a state of being whereby the TLCs are in continuous alignment between balanced values and their vision. By knowing that they are on the path toward achieving that vision or that goal and honoring what they value the most, they become empowered individuals of people who are walking toward their goal with an unwavering belief that they can reach their destination. Because, at every single step they take, they are already there. They become confident that they are on the right path toward their vision, that they are allowed to honor what is most valuable to them, that their values are aligned with that of the organization and team, and that they belong to an empowered group. The TLCs reflect that gratitude to others and therefore empower them in the process even more as it amplifies the sense of appreciation.

Being grateful includes a sense of appreciation by recognizing the efforts, contributions, and achievements of others. Gratitude and appreciation reflect the maturity of the business and a good attitude becomes essential for building a happy working environment. The reason why we mention a happy working environment is that happiness is the highest level of engagement. When people are engaged and aligned, they are highly motivated. They feel that they belong to the organization or the environment so it becomes their natural habitat. Therefore, they are happy. Research has proven that when team members are in a happy environment, they perform at a much higher level than they do in any other environment. One study, published in the Journal of Applied Psychology[12], found that happy employees are more likely to engage in creative problem-solving, which can lead to innovation and improved performance. The study surveyed employees from a variety of industries and found that those who reported higher levels of happiness were more likely to come up with innovative solutions to problems.

Another study[13] by Gallup found that teams with higher employee engagement have 21% higher productivity and 22% higher profitability than those with lower engagement levels. Employee engagement is closely tied to employee happiness, as engaged employees are more likely to feel a sense of purpose and fulfillment in their work.

By reflecting gratitude, they are reflecting kindness which supports other people by extending gratitude to every element within the organization. They contribute to their self-esteem, productivity, and resilience. All of these attributes become a reflection of a strong organization that acts as the main driver for creating a positive workforce or a positive working environment.

If we look at the true essence of gratitude, it can be defined as the positive emotion felt after receiving something valuable. Imagine a TLC interacting with the team or the environment within the organization while always reflecting gratitude by sending positive emotions as a sign of appreciation for something good received from or perceived in others. This directly contributes to the well-being of the team and raises their self-esteem which will partake in their self-confidence and belief in what they are doing. This also raises their motivation to give even more.

There are four ways for leaders to become TLCs to manifest the mindset of gratitude:

i. Focusing on people before performance;
ii. Customizing their way of giving thanks to others;
iii. Being specific about what they are being grateful for; and
iv. Being authentic in showing gratitude.

Studies[14] show that when we express gratitude toward ourselves or others we experience a higher level of the hormone oxytocin, which is usually associated with social bonding and happiness.

One such study was conducted by researchers at the University of California, Los Angeles (UCLA) and was published in the journal Psychological Science in 2007. In this study, participants were randomly assigned to one of three groups: a gratitude expression group, a neutral events group, or a negative events group. The gratitude group was instructed to write a letter expressing gratitude to someone who had positively impacted their life, while the other two groups were instructed to write about neutral or negative events.

The researchers found that participants in the gratitude group reported feeling more positive emotions and feeling more socially connected to others than participants in the other groups. They also found that participants in the gratitude group had significantly higher levels of oxytocin than participants in the other groups. This suggests that expressing gratitude can have a positive impact on social bonding and happiness through its effect on oxytocin levels.

Therefore, by reflecting on gratitude, we contribute to the physical well-being of others and ourselves. By expressing gratitude, leaders send a message to everyone that they are appreciative beyond what words can express.

If gratitude is that great, why don't leaders everywhere embrace and reflect on it? Unfortunately, gratitude is misunderstood. Some people see it as a sign of weakness, in the same way, they misunderstand vulnerability. Gratitude is a sign of strength, and it leads to a much stronger organization. Gratitude reinforces the qualities of self-control, patience, and honesty, all of which are important to self-mastery. It contributes to their capacity to postpone immediate gratification, and therefore, develop stronger willpower. When embraced as a mental state, gratitude empowers the TLCs and the organization as a whole.

2. Bliss: The second pillar in the TLC mindset is blissful thinking, or being in a state of happiness and joy, fostering a contented working environment that comes from an internal belief or perception about the surroundings. Living in a state of happiness enables the person to open up, connect, and be in a state of focus where nothing else matters. Productivity and efficiency are enhanced as a result of that state.

In his book, Dr. Csikszentmihalyi the creator of the flow model[15], mentions that the key to happiness lies in how we invest our psychic energy. When we focus our attention consciously or unconsciously on a chosen goal, our psychic energy flows in the direction of that goal, resulting in reordering and harmony within our consciousness. He defines flow as a state in which people are so deeply involved in an activity that nothing else seems to matter. If the experience is enjoyable, people will redesign their lives to do it, even at a greater cost, just for the sheer rewarding sense of achievement. He then identified the different elements involved in achieving flow, which is clear goals every step of the way, directly feeding back to one's actions, and with a balance between challenges, skills, actions, and awareness. This means that instead of pushing people to work hard to get results, leaders need to focus on facilitating a happy work environment, a fulfilling one, meaning that leaders need to put their effort to assign their team members to tasks they would self-motivate to achieve, and that will provide them a positive challenge to stretch their capacity.

This empowers the team and enables them to connect and go the extra mile to be effective, simply because they are working on those goals, which for them is contributing to a higher objective which is maintaining the happiness of the whole organization.

THE TRANSCENDENCE LEADER-COACH MINDSET

"If you are pained by external things, it is not that they disturb you, but your judgment of them. And it is your power to wipe out that judgment now."

— MARCUS AURELIUS[16]

Again, if bliss is so powerful, then why aren't most businesses embracing it? The main reason why businesses are not working on internal happiness and bliss is that most leaders do not understand its reality, and are unable to do what is needed to realize it. For leaders to establish that, they need to understand the essence of bliss, and how happiness connects to it in creating a positive work environment which leads to better results, embed it in their mindset, and start taking action to instill it in the organization.

3. Abundance: The third pillar of the TLC mindset is abundance, or having the belief that there are plenty of possibilities. Everything is available out there, but they have just not achieved it yet. The belief that opportunities and solutions are available has to be aligned internally. It's not the leaders' job alone to find those opportunities and to work for them; rather, it is about connecting with others who are part of that abundance, invoking their wisdom, and connecting it to harness the collective wisdom of the group. This can only happen when leaders build relationships based on trust and empowerment. That's why a coach's mindset is so empowering because it is based on the fact that "clients are naturally creative, resourceful, and whole." They, therefore, believe that ideas and solutions are abundant and they trust others to have the potential within to find them and be creative and innovative. Coaches hold the space to facilitate the process for others to tap into their inner potential, they do not provide the answers. TLCs give others the chance to find their own answers as part of empowerment while supporting them.

Dealing with others based on the belief that they are "creative, resourceful, and whole" is empowering. If we study successful people who started from scratch, we can see that one common feature among them is an abundance mindset: they face challenges with the belief that there are many opportunities that can be grabbed. Embracing an abundance mindset means that leaders lead from a place of possibility, appreciation, and belief that everyone needs to evolve. There is no envy across an organization in which an abundance mindset is fostered since it is driven by a belief that there is enough to go around.

Abundance drives how leaders move in the world based on being fulfilled and confident as to where they can reach. Their perspective, as leaders, to matters which arise is one of opportunity, instead of challenges. In turn, this fosters a sense of stability and belief within the organization. When people look at the future with abundance, it shows them that opportunities exist which is reflected in job security, progression, and growth, in turn leading to more positivity within the organization.

Imagine if every conversation in the organization begins with "where can we be? and what's the positive impact of being there?" rather than discussing the potential shortcomings!

THE TRANSCENDENCE LEADER-COACH MINDSET

Unfortunately, in reality, when challenges appear, most organizations' immediate discussions are about how to cut costs, how to reduce manpower, and how to achieve efficiency based on cutting on investments. This is a paradigm of scarcity that is reflected in reduced contributions from the team. Having a true abundance mindset does not mean that leaders need to cover their eyes to the harshness of the truth, but rather look at the reality of the world with an outlook or belief that if they are grounded and can look through ambiguity, there is an opportunity beyond the current challenge that needs exploring. Having a mindset of abundance fosters growth based on collaboration.

Leaders who believe that creativity is abundant within the organization will take action to break down silos, create bridges of communication, and start creating dynamic cross-functional connections between teams to increase the level of dialogue based on a belief in one another. This in itself sends a message across the organization whereby all team members can sense their value, and therefore reciprocate that mindset by being connected even more to the organization and to the goals and putting in the extra mile. Leaders can practice developing abundance by acting on these three steps:

i. First, embracing the curiosity of a coach by being curious about everything. Approach matters with a sense of wonder or bewilderment, seeking solutions from a basis of positivity and appreciation by asking questions such as: "How can we make it happen? What can we change or how can we evolve so that we can achieve what we aspire to?"

ii. Second, increasing the number of abundance-minded people within the organization. Make it a part of your objective as you become a Transcendence Leader-Coach by passing that culture and message across all levels of the organization. You need to surround yourself with people with mutual beliefs.
iii. And last, practicing shifting perspectives. Whenever possible, try to see things from another angle, and lean into that new perspective. See what you can appreciate by looking through another lens. Look at change as an adventure and embrace failure as an opportunity for growth.

4. Positivity: Positivity as a mindset is how leaders approach unpleasantness or unpleasant events in a more productive way that opens the door for more creative thinking and hope. Positivity is not about deceiving themselves that everything is great; it is about seeing the challenges and embracing them, believing that they can work on them in a productive way that will yield positive results.

> *"Sooner or later, those who win are those who think they can."*
>
> – PAUL TOURNIER

Positivity is the belief that "they can." There are no guaranteed results; however, there is a belief from the leaders that "they can" overcome certain challenges. By focusing on positive thinking, they can turn negative thoughts into positive ones. It's a simple process, but it takes time and practice. Some of the areas where leaders can shift to applying positive thinking are:

i. First, identifying the areas of change. Therefore, they need to understand which areas they tend to perceive negatively.
ii. Second, check-in what's supporting their negative perception.
iii. Third, follow a healthy routine in responding to challenges, and how to share them with the team. This routine includes the way they discuss and invite the team to share creative solutions, sending the message that they can contribute too.

Positive leadership supports the idea that focusing on the team's growth and potential takes place by shifting their focus toward what can be (the potential), by eliminating obstacles that are a major barrier to their effectiveness. Positive leadership requires embracing a positive mindset, free from criticism and judgment, exactly like coaches. While sitting with clients, coaches listen without judgment or analysis and listen objectively with curiosity and appreciation for what might show up; listening with the belief that whatever shows up can be explored and that clients can transform challenges and adversities into opportunities that might yield better results. To maintain a positive mindset, leaders should focus on strengths rather than weaknesses. This doesn't mean that they ignore negativity or weakness, but they emphasize the existing positivity. This can be amplified by always remembering when they take the positive route, what the outcome is, and how it positively impacts the environment.

Similarly, in a coaching relationship, coaches will tend to focus on what is positive because positivity yields possibility. Positivity creates hope and hope opens up the minds of other people, allowing them to think differently and creatively simply because they believe that there is a solution. People who think negatively tend to have a closed mindset. They think that there is no hope, and there is no solution, so why should they try to think of a way forward? Their brains focus only on amplifying the negative and all they see are roadblocks. Positive teams are always productive teams.

Positivity by itself creates resilience because, the hope it provides, gives people the motivation to continue to try to move forward with the belief that they know they can reach that destination. Positivity also yields optimism, and optimism by itself will yield problem-solving capability. So, members who are involved in such an environment tend to be better at problem-solving and report less frustration. By embracing positivity, TLCs provide unity for the team because it brings them closer to each other. There is a unifying factor, a belief that they can reach where they want to reach. They always listen to each other without barriers or judgment, and therefore the environment becomes open for growth and prosperity. For leaders to transcend to becoming TLCs, they should walk the path of positivity by embracing:

- ❖ Integrity;
- ❖ Self-esteem;
- ❖ Self-efficacy;
- ❖ Resilience;

- Gratitude; and
- Self-care

All of these combined can create a sense of unwavering positivity within the leaders, and therefore, transform the team.

5. Growth: The fifth pillar in the TLC mindset is growth. Growth is about empowering others and fostering collaboration and innovation and not about looking smart. It is about taking a path of continuous development to learn and evolve on the path to success. When leaders embrace a growth mindset, they are embracing the belief that everyone can grow and evolve. At the core of growth, there should be trust: trusting in one's ability and that of others to grow. One way that can support a growth mindset is by embarking on positive challenges that can stretch the capacity of the team. Leaders can support the team and the organization to grow faster by offering the team the chance to work on specific challenges that are assigned in relation to the team's capability.

The "Flow Model" created by Dr. Csikszentmihalyi, says that if leaders provide a challenge that is greater than the ability of the team, the team will start to feel pressure, leading to burnout and anxiety. If leaders present a challenge that is way lower than their capability, they will start developing apathy and complacency. So, to maintain a balance, leaders who believe in the growth capacity of the team will have to explore the potential of that team first, like a coach explores the inner potential of clients.

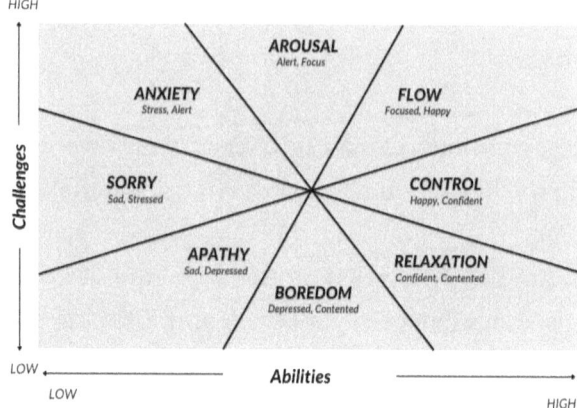

FIGURE 6.2: THE FLOW MODEL

This reminds me of the king in *The Little Prince* by Antoine de Saint-Exupery[17]. "If I ordered a general to fly from one flower to another like a butterfly, or to write a tragic drama, or to change himself into a sea bird, and if the general did not carry out the order that he had received, which one of us would be in the wrong?" the king demanded. "The general, or myself?"

"You," said the little prince firmly.

"Exactly. One must require from each one the duty which each one can perform," the king went on. "Accepted authority rests first of all on reason. If you ordered your people to go and throw themselves into the sea, they would rise up in revolution. I have the right to require obedience because my orders are reasonable."

THE TRANSCENDENCE LEADER-COACH MINDSET

If we draw an analogy with coaching, we see that coaches first believe that everyone has the capacity to grow, and they have the potential to do so even though they don't see it at that point. Coaches support exploring and identifying hidden potential and focusing on growing that potential. From there, they enable people to shift their perspectives on the challenges they face. Similarly, to foster a growth environment, leaders should share opportunities with the team, listen to them, and collaborate with them on setting goals and planning the way forward. Eloquent leaders, and in this case TLCs, have the capacity to articulate challenges in a way that seems inviting to the team. By stretching the team within their capability and a little beyond, leaders will not create stress; but will be creating an environment of development that is going to yield better results for future leaders in the making. A growth mindset supports a positive mindset, and vice versa.

Having a growth mindset affects the lens through which leaders process information and select what information will serve the organization moving forward. It acts as a guide or a navigation system for leaders in having a broader horizon with a belief that there is the capacity to evolve and forge new paths to reach their goals. When leaders try to transcend to achieve the TLC approach, they embrace a growth mindset because of various reasons that contribute to people's development:

i. First, growth means that leaders value the people around them and believe in them by providing them the chance to develop as a sign that they truly matter.

ii. Second, it increases the number of people who "can"; therefore, it has a multiplier effect within the organization.
iii. Third, it has a rewarding effect on the team through making them feel a sense of achievement by having an opportunity to contribute.
iv. Fourth, it answers the aspirations of people as they aspire to grow. As human beings, one of our main drivers is to grow mentally, not only in the sense of age or position but at the mental level.
v. Finally, it contributes to creativity and innovation because it is through growth that people see a path that will push them to think differently and to create a new way forward.

Disruption: Shaking the Paradigm

One main way for leaders to embrace a growth mindset is to take the path of disruption. Disrupting the self means shaking the internal paradigms to move out of the comfort zone by thinking differently. This will light the spark of innovation within leaders and the organization. By developing a growth mindset, leaders will be preparing themselves and the team - and therefore the organization - for change.

In preparing for that change, leaders will have to ask a few important questions that come from a growth mindset by looking at the current practices and behaviors the team and organization are involved in that need to be shaken:

i. What has worked earlier for us and is no longer working? We need to think and re-envision the way we do things.
ii. How much time are we spending on creative cycles or creative engagements?
iii. What can we do more to develop our current capacities about where we are heading?

Recognizing the Team's Efforts

Another aspect that leaders need to set in place to ensure the growth mindset continues within the organization is recognizing the contribution of the team. Recognizing the efforts of the team will send a clear message across the organization that they truly care and appreciate those who go the extra mile and are ready to lead. Leaders embracing a growth mindset will also ensure learning comes from any failures experienced. This means approaching each failure with an open discussion with the team, so that people can identify the key learnings from their mistakes because mistakes are looked at as opportunities for growth.

6. Forward-Thinking: The sixth pillar of the TLC mindset is forward thinking which means being connected to the present while having an eye on the future. It is about embracing change and mastering the art of adaptation as a fact of life while adapting to the new reality. In this sense, the art of adaptation is the art of evolution because we are evolving rather than staying where we are. TLCs have a forward-thinking approach. They have a clear vision and are driven by a clear statement of why they do what they do, and what it means for them to achieve what they want to achieve.

The main goal of TLCs is to develop an organizational environment that is full of extraordinary leaders. To have the team think of their future selves as extraordinary leaders, they have to develop a forward-thinking mindset that can be engraved in the organization by having a clear sense of direction and a culture that is clear on its vision and aware of the mission that will lead to that vision. TLCs can create a forward-thinking capacity by involving the team in deciphering that vision not as a one-time exercise, but as a continuous engagement throughout the year by engaging them to see how they are evolving in their understanding of that vision, and what they can contribute by having new ways to translate into reality.

The pressures of day-to-day work make it easy for leaders to get sucked-in by operational matters. To transcend to the TLC approach, leaders need to assign time to break out of the operational cycle and look at the organization from the outside:

1. Expand their thinking capacity;
2. Strengthen the muscle of innovation;
3. Tap into insights outside the organization;
4. Involve the team in areas outside the scope of the organization, within the industry and sometimes in other industries; and

5. Look at the evolving technology trends in the industry and the type of business that can be initiated by looking at discussions that can fortify the business in the organization.

Forward-thinking leaders are by nature positive. They use their positivity to articulate their outlook in an inspiring manner that allows everyone to see more clearly what their vision stands for and what it looks like. In other words, TLCs can enable others to see their vision in a formed manner, and therefore, allow them to sense it, feel it, and touch the tangible aspects of that vision, which makes it more believable and achievable in their perception.

Engage the Team in a Feed-Forward Conversation

One way that TLCs can fortify a forward-thinking approach is by transforming the type of conversations that happen with team members. Instead of providing feedback, they engage in feed-forward conversations. A feed-forward conversation doesn't dwell too much on the past as a key learning for growth, but rather puts the objective and the goal at the center of the discussion. The idea is to learn from mistakes, be accountable, and yet look at the way forward and how we can recoup what has been lost. Feed-forward is an ongoing discussion while the team is working toward the goal.

It is reported that in all performance discussions, when leaders start focusing on the future rather than focusing on what went wrong in the past the team becomes more positive. They start engaging in the performance discussion in a fair way where they start assessing themselves before the leader assesses them, and start looking internally as to what they can improve and enhance because talking about it in a forward manner shows the team that the leader still considers them as part of the team moving forward, still appreciates the strengths they have without focusing on their weaknesses. So, forward-thinking leaders will not focus on the obstacles (though they will see obstacles and identify them), but on what will happen when they overcome the obstacles. The belief that there is something beyond those obstacles will drive people's creativity and innovation on ways to overcome those obstacles.

The conversation within the organization transforms to become more of a visionary talk rather than talking about the past, and while talking about the future it naturally focuses on what is happening in the "Now" moment and not the past. Because the team cannot change the past, however they can have the chance to shape the future by what they decide today. The team will realize that their decisions in the now moment has the chance to become actions that will shape the future. Similarly, coaches sit across from the clients and initiate that forward-thinking through powerful questions that facilitate a creative thinking process focusing on what's positive and what's possible, which means looking at what the clients want to achieve and what their vision of the future is. By that token, leaders need to lean into the coaches' approach by leading through powerful questions that are forward-driven, positively charged, and focused on what is possible.

Committing to a Continuous Outlook

Another component of forward-thinking is commitment. Forward-thinking leaders try to change the environment around them. They walk the talk by committing to a continuous future-focused outlook that reflects their enthusiasm to realize that vision. The team around the leaders will relate to this behavior and will be empowered to lead the change because, based on the clarity of their vision, they can see where they are heading.

Evolution Barriers

Change, evolution, and prosperity can only happen by embracing the NOW moment and being clear that what leaders decide now, shapes the future. It is the quality of their thinking that either fosters growth, creativity, and innovation or holds back any effort that is made by the team. Leaders impact all levels within the organization. It is the leaders' mindset that cascades down through the organization. However, leaders have to rewire their mental processes, break away from previous habits, and start holding a new perspective and a more human-centric approach to leadership. The old way of knowing it all and feeling the pressure of always providing the answers is limiting. It is based on a combination of EGO and unacknowledged FEAR which acts the opposite of the intended objective. Ego limits humans' capability to connect with others or to build on their potential. It limits their ability to see clearly, while fear stops them from going forward. It is the biggest barrier to change and evolution.

So far, we have established the six pillars of a coach's mindset that need to be embraced by all leaders to be ready to manifest the competencies of a TLC:

1. Gratitude, and its impact on recognizing efforts;
2. Bliss, in its power to bring happiness to the work environment as an indicator of engagement;
3. Abundance, with its capacity to open new horizons;
4. Positivity, and its ability to fuel belief in self and team;
5. Growth, and the motivation it gives others when leaders believe in their capacity; and
6. Forward-thinking, with the power to envision the future.

My invitation to you is to allow yourself the time to reflect and see where you stand in relation to these six pillars and what you need to do to embrace them. We all carry with us old habits, some of which may have served us in the past; however, it's always good to reassess our approach and check-in what the frame of reference supporting our approach is. What mindset do we have now, and how can we embrace a different mindset? How can we integrate what is missing from the 6 pillars of the Transcendence Leader-Coach's mindset? My invitation to you is to reflect and raise your self-awareness and identify opportunities to instill the 6 pillars and act upon them, which will facilitate implementing the 16 core competencies of the TLC that we shall cover in the upcoming chapters.

Questions to reflect on:

- ❖ Gratitude:
    - What are the three things that I am grateful for today and why? How do these things have positively impacted my life and why they are meaningful to me?
    - In what ways can I express gratitude towards someone who has positively impacted my life?
    - What specific actions can I take, to show my appreciation, and how these actions will benefit both me, and the person I am expressing gratitude towards?
- ❖ Bliss:
    - What does "bliss" mean to me, and how do I experience it in my life?
    - What beliefs or behaviors might be blocking me from experiencing more bliss in my life? (Reflect on any limiting beliefs or self-sabotaging behaviors that might be holding you back from experiencing more joy and fulfillment, and brainstorm ways to overcome these obstacles and invite more bliss into your life).
    - How can i reflect bliss on the team?
- ❖ Abundance:
    - In what areas of my life do I feel abundant? (Reflect on the areas of your life where you feel fulfilled and abundant, such as relationships, career, health, or personal

growth, and consider how you can amplify these areas of abundance in your life).
- In what ways might scarcity mindset be holding me back from experiencing abundance in my life? (Reflect on any limiting beliefs or negative self-talk that might be causing you to feel scarcity in certain areas of your life, and consider how you can shift your mindset to one of abundance and gratitude. Brainstorm actions you can take to cultivate a more abundant mindset and attract more abundance into your life).

❖ Positivity:
- How do I typically respond to negative situations or challenges in my life? (Reflect on your default thought patterns and behaviors when faced with adversity, and consider how you can shift towards a more positive and resilient mindset. What strategies can you use to reframe negative situations and find the positive in them?)
- Who are the people in my life who bring positivity and joy, and how can I cultivate more positive relationships?
- When was the last time I reframed a negative situation into a positive one?

❖ Growth:
- In what areas of my life do I feel most called to grow or develop?
- What limiting beliefs or behaviors might be holding me back from experiencing growth and fulfillment in my life?
- What actions did I take to grow the team?

- ❖ Forward thinking?
  - What is one area of my life where I want to see significant progress or change in the next year?
  - What might be holding me back from thinking more proactively? What new habits or mindsets can I adopt to become more proactive and intentional in shaping my future?

The 6 TLC Mindset Pillars Action Plan

Reflect on your actions and write down in each category 3 actions that will drive you closer to the best version of yourself as a Transcendence Leader-Coach.

KEEP DOING	START DOING	STOP DOING

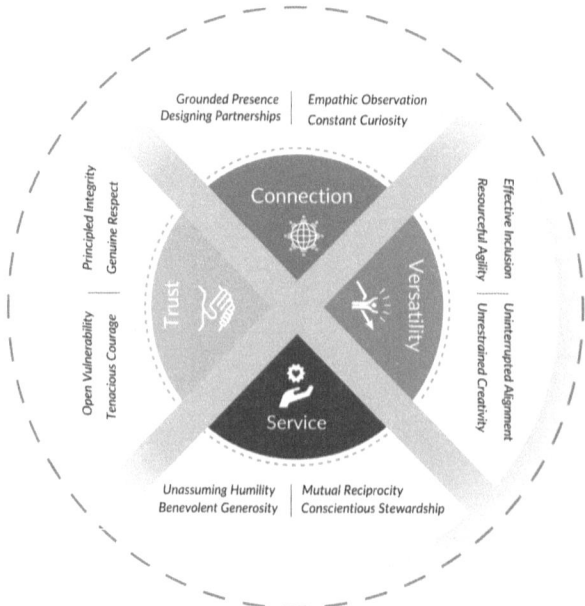

FIGURE 7.1: TLC COMPETENCY FRAMEWORK

7

BUILDING BRIDGES

First Cluster: Connection

"Connection, is the energy that is created between people when they feel seen, heard, and valued. When they can give and receive without judgement."

— BRENE BROWN[18]

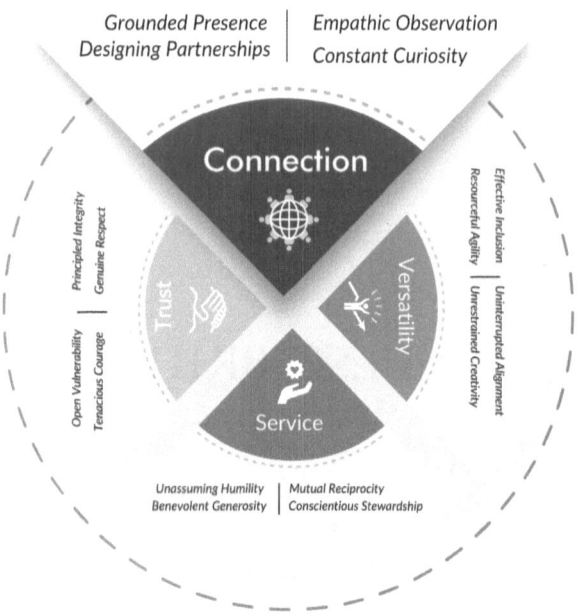

FIGURE 7.2: CONNECTION CLUSTER

The deepest connections I was able to witness across the various environments and especially in the ASEAN region were those built around compassion and empathy. What seemed to be a soft approach turned out to be a strong, deep leadership approach, building connections that enabled partnerships based on presence and empathy while being fueled by curiosity. Being present in the moment and witnessing others connecting to what was being said and not said enabled leaders to create that environment and sense underlying changes through connecting with others and caring for them. This care developed a sense of engagement, belonging, and loyalty. Every team I have interviewed and interacted with by having friendly talks, apart from our usual business dealings, showed me that their leaders manifest understanding (empathy), caring with an intention to resolve (compassion), and curiosity to engage with the team created the sense that each team member was important, no matter what their role in the business was.

This was the inspiration for me to apply the same rationale with my team by coaching them, cascading this culture down through all levels which created a change that enabled a breakthrough across 2,300 associates who were willing to give more with a smile.

We live in a world of connection. People are social beings who thrive on connection. Our health is greatly affected by the quality of connections that we form. Neuroscience research has proven the negative impact of the lack of connection with others and highlighted the negative impact of harmful relations among people to an extent that can result in illness. The research also shows that most employees call in sick when they experience negative interactions with others[19].

A study published in the International Journal of Business and Management found that workplace incivility, which includes rude or disrespectful behavior from colleagues, is a significant predictor of employee absenteeism. The study surveyed employees from various industries and found that those who experienced workplace incivility were more likely to miss work. Similarly, a study published in the Journal of Occupational Health Psychology found that workplace bullying, which includes verbal abuse and humiliation, was associated with higher levels of absenteeism. These studies suggest that negative interactions with others in the workplace can have a negative impact on employee attendance.

When we talk about connection, we talk about building bridges with team members, peers, and leadership within the organization. The first question that leaders should ask candidly is, "What does my team know about me?" Answering this question is not about the team members knowing the name or position of the leader, but about knowing what leaders stand for, advocate, and believe in.

The second question is, "Do I know the people I work with?" This question should be answered to the same extent as knowing one's self, especially when identifying whether the leaders know their team's goals, aspirations, what they value, what they care for, and whom their family is made up of. Do they know them as individuals, for the person they are, the "who" in them and not as emplyees only? By building connections between people, the team starts to understand that the leaders are actually standing beside them and not against them. One of the main things that drives the four competencies within this cluster (Grounded Presence, Empathetic Observation, Constant Curiosity, and Designing Partnerships) is the belief that leaders should build emotional compensation within the organization.

Emotional Compensation

Emotional compensation supports the seven universal human needs of respect, recognition, belonging, autonomy, personal growth, meaning, and progress. One more need can be added to that list which is self-actualization. By supporting those universal needs, leaders create a positive emotion across the organization and the team through the power of connection. Connection is a key to commitment, and commitment is the bond that holds the team together around a common goal to achieve the vision of the organization, or the shared vision of the whole group.

One challenge which is being researched across the world is the impact of disconnection that people experience when they lose their social bonds and their social connections with each other. This challenge was taken on by leaders in learning how to build connections remotely. Some research found that employees who experience high levels of belonging change jobs less often, have increased job performance, less reported sick leave, and have an increase in total employer promoter scores. One study published in the Journal of Occupational Health Psychology[20] found that social support from co-workers was negatively related to turnover intention, meaning that employees who perceived high levels of social support from their colleagues were less likely to consider leaving their job. The study also found that social support was positively related to job satisfaction and work engagement, and negatively related to emotional exhaustion.

The way to build connections is by looking at the types of relationships leaders are building in an organization. One of the better relationships to build is friendship relationship based on trust and appreciation which will lead to further job satisfaction.

Friendship

Friendship relationships does not mean sacrificing accountability or the sense of responsibility within the organization. A mature friendship-relationship means that people understand their roles and obligations in the relationship, yet there is no reason for them not to enjoy it while working toward those obligations. The invitation for leaders to emulate the TLC is to provide enough time to build connections across the organization. Leaders should spend time in the hallways of the organization or society, observing and listening to how people behave and what they talk about, what they say, and what they don't say. By doing so, they start sending the right message: that they care. By taking a step forward to inquire about what employees say or how they behave or what they feel, leaders anchor that message by showing that they truly care. Listening to people and checking how they are is one of the highest signs of respect and of inviting others to belong. One additional step that can anchor that effort is following up. It's not enough to ask and listen or inquire; what is important is to follow up with people on what leaders have inquired about and get them into partnership by applying what has shown-up during the conversation.

In coaching, this is called follow-through. Coaches will follow through on what shows up in the conversation and what best serves the clients and not their (the coaches) own agenda. This reflects a genuine relationship that enhances the connection between the coaches and the clients. Follow-through reflects curiosity and genuine care to what the other person is saying, and when coupled with action this reflects a genuine intention to build on that partnership.

A Coaching Relationship

If we are to draw an analogy with coaching, coaches who start a coaching conversation with clients first and foremost focus on the person behind the conversation, the "who" and not the topic. Coaches are interested in building a partnership and a connection in a coaching relationship based on trust and safety by being objective, empathetic listeners who are curious about what the other person is saying. This curiosity drives the questions by which the coaches inquire and probe to evoke further awareness for the client. If there is no connection between the coach and the client, the relationship will break at some point in time. If the client will not open up, the relationship will not be authentic.

The coaching relationship itself is an invitation for people to belong in the space where they are being listened to, and where they are allowed to explore their belief systems and emotions. It is a safe space where they can explore things they have not explored in any other kind of conversation, even with their closest friends. This is part of why coaching has been successful in providing sustainable impact and sustainable results. So, our invitation to leaders is to become TLCs who are able to foster connection-building across the organization and ensure that it becomes a habit and part of the culture itself by transforming discussions to coaching conversations.

In her book, *The Business of Friendship*[21], Shasta Nelson talks about three essential things in friendship to thrive:

- positivity, to feel satisfied;
- vulnerability, to feel safe; and
- consistency, to feel seen.

Positivity refers to the feelings of satisfaction that come from spending time with friends who have a positive outlook on life. **Vulnerability** is about feeling safe to share one's authentic self with friends, without fear of judgment or rejection. **Consistency** means that friends regularly make time for each other, which helps individuals feel seen and valued in their relationships. By prioritizing these elements in our friendships, we can create more meaningful and fulfilling connections in our lives.

Providing that kind of consistency by making "building connections" a habit, will open up the space for the rest of the organization to do the same. Another way for leaders to build connections is to ask for support. By doing so, they are breaking down walls by showing vulnerability, those imaginary walls which have been built by the idea that leaders lead by authority. Doing so in a consistent manner, they send an immediate message that they are approachable. The team will then feel they can ask for support as well because they trust the leader who came to them for that purpose. The leader seeking support helps to bring down false images of authority and build connections based on trust and openness.

Another invitation to leaders, which will be seen more in all organizations in the future, is to allow or actually support team members to spend more time with their families, and take care of their loved ones. When they feel enriched and satisfied in that area, the team will directly connect that satisfaction with its source, the facilitator, the leader of the organization. The organization is no longer seen as taking the team away from what they love and what they like to do. The organization and the leader will be viewed as a source of motivation and inspiration, allowing them to do what they love to do, and therefore the connection will become stronger.

As mentioned, building connection stands on four competencies: Grounded Presence, Empathetic Observation, Constant Curiosity, and Designing partnerships.

Competency One: Grounded Presence

Presence is being there, but it is the quality of being which is most important. Leaders who are present are comfortable, humble, and engaged. They are present in the moment, aware of what's happening around them, and able to translate that into an engagement with the team. They are friendly and approachable because they are intentional about their presence and they want their presence to be felt. They speak with clarity and respect in the sense of determination or belief because they make every second count in their presence. In many aspects, presence is the ability to connect with others. It's not about charisma or the image they project, but rather it is about their ability to connect to different people at the individual level as much as at the professional level.

Presence is amplified by self-awareness. As mentioned earlier, the multi-dimensional awareness that leaders should have amplifies their presence. Starting with self-awareness, leaders should have an understanding of personality traits, habits, abilities, and behaviors, and be aware of how these impact others in the work environment. Self-aware leaders are conscious of their choice of words and actions and consider the impact on people around them before they act or speak. They reflect on their own thoughts, words, and actions, observe themselves and others and see the impact of their actions and interconnected actions within the environment. They step forward in supporting or mending any negative impact. They are empathetic by being understanding of others and they translate that into listening to understand, rather than to judge. They are highly responsive because they are in the moment and they realize and notice things as they happen, and are able to engage their team and the environment around them in the moment. They are humble and approachable, and they don't perceive leadership as tied to their position. They draw strength from the connections they have with others and with the team. They exert a high sense of self-management; therefore, they are not carried away by their emotions. They ensure that their presence is felt and is not affected by their thoughts or personal matters that concern them.

This creates a profound impact on others as they feel important and valued as a result of such presence that is directed toward them. Feeling valued empowers team members and gives them the courage to take action and the responsibility to reciprocate such presence with focus. A focus that will make them more engaged, dedicated and efficient.

Competency Two: Empathetic Observation

In creating any coaching conversation, coaches need to build a partnership, and that partnership is built on presence. Coaches need to be grounded in the moment and not distracted by self or anything else. Coaches believe that they are there to witness the clients' transformation. They are reflective in their own mindset, and this translates itself through the coaches' reflective questions which deepens the learning for the clients and evokes further awareness. Coaches hold no perspective, no judgment, and instead notice what is said and not said and act as a sounding board for the clients.

What drives the coaches' observation and listening is empathy. It is the ability to understand without judgment and without interrupting the client. As a profession or a skill, coaching becomes essential for any leader who is focusing on transcending beyond the normal leadership approach or status. Empathetic leadership means having the ability to understand the needs of others. It is being aware of where those needs come from without judgment, understanding and appreciating the differences among people and their backgrounds. Empathetic leadership means that they are focused on the other person so that they are more human-centric which will eventually drive their ability to be compassionate and to connect with others, both on the personal and professional level.

Competency Three: Constant Curiosity

Without curiosity, there is little drive for leaders to explore and learn new things, and little motivation to build on, step forward, and try to understand others. Without being motivated to understand others, leaders will not be motivated to build connections with them. So, to build proper connections, leaders have to amplify their curiosity toward others. The curious mind learns about people, connects better with them, and inspires a creative thinking process. In neuroscience, curiosity is acknowledged as being one of the oldest cognitive pathways. It is well-ingrained in the human's brain and it is effective as well. By tapping into curiosity, humans initiate the creative power of the brain, thus rewarding self and others. Curiosity is when leaders shift the focus from themselves toward others which allows other people to feel that they are important and interesting.

> *"I sat with the manager and I felt that he is important. While I sat with the leader, I felt that I am important."*
>
> – Anonymous

TLCs know how to manage themselves and control their ego drive. This is part of them being humble. They support people to understand themselves and explore their inner potential so that they can stand on their own and move forward on firmer ground, and thus will no longer need to depend on their leader or on anyone else.

Curiosity is a tool for empowerment that coaches express through questions. It is the element that drives the quality of the questions coaches ask which shapes the quality of the conversations that follow. It starts with the mindset that coaches embrace: that it's not about the coach, but about the other person, and that they are going to have an enriching relationship. Coaches should approach the relationship with an open mind, with a full authentic belief that understanding others yields better learning, and this will shape the coaches' capacity to listen and understand with an eagerness to learn more. This will encourage coaches to start making powerful inquiries to drive people to open up, expand, identify their potential, and feel safe and worthy of doing so. Leaders embracing a coach's curiosity will have an approach that always seeks to notice what's important for the other person, thus cultivating the cognitive ability and mental capacity of the team by simply providing them the chance to think differently. In that sense, leaders are evoking the creativity and innovation cycle within the team.

The biggest value that curiosity can bring to organizations is opening up the chance for more meaningful conversations based on appreciation and understanding. This triggers the collective wisdom of the group which in turn supports leaders and organizations. Developing new ideas and problem solving is no longer on leaders alone. The key is coupling curiosity with a sense of respect and safety so that the other person does not see the leaders' inquiry as an interrogation. Once respect and safety are present, people will see such inquiry as an invitation and they will be open to accepting the invitation and be drawn into a new level of relationship with leaders.

In a conversation that arises out of curiosity, there is no room for ego, arrogance, or judgment. There is no room for the leaders' cognitive biases. It's about setting aside what they know so that they can welcome what they don't know. Curiosity that is based on interest in the other person is also a sign of courage. Curiosity in itself allows the level of conversation to transcend to a higher level by being present, connected "in the moment" and maintaining the self-control that opens up their capacity to listen to people empathetically and without judgment. This in itself fosters their curiosity to learn more, to learn neutrally, and to ask further questions which leads to developing a solid partnership.

Competency Four: Designing Partnerships

Building partnerships is the highest level of connection because they can only be formed on a basis of trust, respect, and equality. To become better leaders, they need to start developing partnerships with others, with people they value and who they believe will add value to the relationship. By inviting people to partner with them on a certain topic in a conversation or project, they empower those connections in the organization. It is not only about building friendships, but also about building empowering relations which add value, and therefore contribute to enhancing productivity.

Partnerships by themselves are empowering as they are based on trust, respect, and autonomy. The relationship involves a value exchange, meaning it is nurturing for both parties because both benefit from the exchange, and both grow. At the core of building a partnership is recognition and appreciation. A partnership is an expression of gratitude toward the other. It recognizes the achievements of other people and their contributions. For leaders to be more effective in building partnerships they need to do as the TLCs do, which is to praise and reciprocate with kindness.

This encourages loyalty and commitment in any relationship. Organizations that build partnerships with their teams based on recognition and appreciation have higher employee engagement, high levels of employee retention, and a high level of efficiency because people are willing to go the extra mile to protect each other and the assets and interests of the organization.

What makes partnerships important is that by forming partnerships leaders gain access to new resources, knowledge, and the capacity to contribute. In the same token, leaders need to build partnerships between team members amongst themselves. Therefore, leaders become a catalyst of trust and confidence among teams and organizations.

Let's look at how all of this comes together. When leaders develop a multi-dimensional awareness, they become grounded and present in the now moment, capable of focusing on each relationship with the team. This presence is felt by others and appreciated, and because people appreciate being given the level of attention they deserve, this facilitates building partnerships. Leaders who are keen on building partnerships focus on influence through trust and respect. Leaders build relationships of equality, not in the sense of forgetting about organizational hierarchy, but in terms of appreciating what each team member has to contribute. Building partnership relations anchors the leaders' sense of empathy because partnerships can't be built without empathetic listening and understanding where the other party is coming from. Empathy by itself fuels curiosity. Having the intention to listen empathetically, listening to understand, makes leaders curious to listen more, understand more, and therefore ask more. Asking makes the team members more engaged, more connected, develops their sense of ownership, and enhances their learning capacity.

> *"Partnerships which are based on trust, respect, and autonomy are nurturing for both parties as they promote growth."*
>
> – IHAB BADAWI

Questions to reflect on:

- What kind of connections have I built around myself?
- How strong are my connections with my team and my peers?
- What is the foundation of my connections?
- How do I show up daily at my work or life?
- When was a time when I felt deeply empathetic toward someone at work? How did I demonstrate that empathy?
- When was the last time I actively sought out someone else's perspective before making a decision? How did it impact my decision-making process?
- Where I may have unintentionally ignored someone else's feelings or needs? How could I have handled that situation differently with empathy?
- How do I make an effort to understand and connect with colleagues who have different backgrounds or perspectives than mine?

- What actions have I taken recently to support the well-being and work-life balance of my team members?
- Have I ever had to deliver difficult news or feedback to an employee? How did I approach the situation with empathy?
- In what ways do I actively practice empathy in my personal life, and how can I apply those practices to my leadership style?
- When did I misunderstand someone else's emotions or intentions? How did I resolve the misunderstanding and build trust moving forward?
- How do I manage my own emotions in high-pressure or conflict situations with colleagues or clients?
- In what ways do I actively listen to and seek out feedback from others to understand their perspectives and needs?
- How curious am I in exploring the world around me?
- When was the last time I actively sought out information or perspectives that challenged my assumptions or beliefs? How did it impact my decision-making process?
- How do I encourage and foster curiosity among my team members? What strategies have I found to be effective in promoting a culture of curiosity?

My Connection Action Plan

Reflect on your actions and write down in each category 3 actions that will drive you closer to the best version of yourself as a Transcendence Leader-Coach.

KEEP DOING	START DOING	STOP DOING

8

THE DOOR TO FLUID LEADERSHIP

Cluster Two: Versatility

"The stiff and unbending is the disciple of death. The gentle and yielding is the disciple of life."

– Lao Tzu[22]

THE RISE OF THE TRANSCENDENCE LEADER-COACH

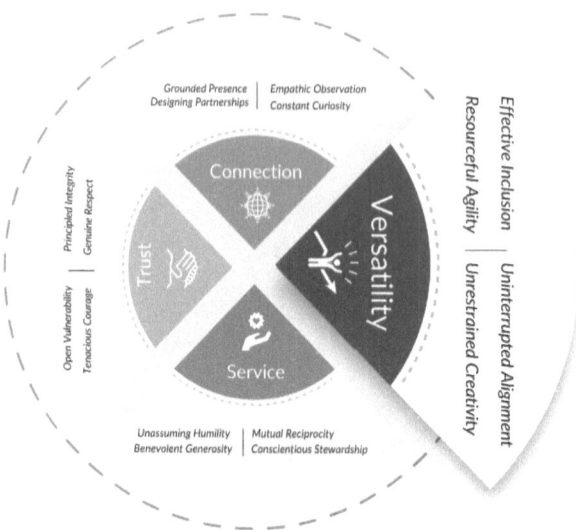

FIGURE 8.1: VERSATILITY CLUSTER

In 1999, I started handling operations dealing with the US market. The relationship with various US counterparts grew from business operations to business transformation. In business operations, the essentials of client service reflect the virtue of versatility. Maintaining a high level of adaptability with a fast response time indicated that there was something much bigger behind it. It was not about the business; it was about how the working culture was built that shaped the people delivering the service. How much they were empowered reflected that versatility.

This piqued my interest to start noticing what kind of leadership is required to build such a culture. It turned out to be that all leaders who were able to build such a culture enjoyed an inclusive mindset that never discarded anyone in the chain. It is by believing that everyone should be heard and has valuable insight, just like a coach operates with undivided attention towards others, that people are invited to be included in the macro formula. This inclusion enabled alignment, with everyone involved, and with the ability to have the chance to express their disagreement in the right context. By being accepting, leaders developed an agile mindset which was easily felt when issues related to business were shared. The ability to respond rapidly to create new solutions, within the limits of a well-crafted policy that enabled creativity, could be felt thousands of miles away.

I asked the head of finance how much the empowerment given to the front liners affected the bottom line. His answer was illuminating: "We recruit responsible thinkers and not executors. We either trust their capability and nurture it or we stay as we are and never grow."

A few years later, when starting my journey to coaching mastery, I came across the same fundamental belief that is the building blocks of coaching: "People are naturally creative resourceful, and whole." Who wouldn't include everyone if they believe in this statement? Leaders who include others, listen to them, and engage with them with curiosity are actually coaching their team members.

In this chapter, we introduce the second cluster, which is versatility. Versatility includes the four competencies of: Effective

Inclusion, Uninterrupted Alignment, Resourceful Agility, and Unrestrained Creativity. Versatility is essential for leaders to have in the sense of being flexible and adaptable. If leaders are not versatile enough to combine all of these competencies in a way that complements each other, then these competencies will not be as effective as they should be. Versatility is the leaders' capacity to bring various competencies together to build on one another. They constitute the ability of those leaders to change. The reason why we always circle back to change is due to the fundamental fact that change, whether from external factors or internal factors, impacts every part of the organization.

TLCs are highly adaptable and capable to evolve. It's not simply accepting the changes as they are, but adapting to the changes: being flexible enough to acquire the new features that come with change, while also having an eye on future changes that will happen. Therefore, while adapting to evolve, the TLCs should be highly flexible, malleable and able to stretch their own horizons, skills, and competencies to accommodate the new skills and competencies, in addition to having a flexible mindset to accept new contributions from others which will provide variety. The TLCs welcome variety with open arms because it adds value. The main pillar for collective wisdom is the summation of the different types of intellect within the organization. Accordingly, variety becomes a goal. It's not the cherry on top, but rather a core aspect that leaders need to include in the team to have an assortment in their strategic thinking, approach, planning, and execution. That's why TLCs will tap into their coaching capacity to evoke that variety from each individual and then use it in a group coaching approach as well so that it can be well integrated within the team.

By definition, having versatility in leaders' perspective means handling different situations and changes that come from all directions. It enables leaders to be grounded within chaos, and to convey a balance from within which will calibrate the chaos around. Versatile leaders are able to continuously adjust behaviors, whether their own or the team's, toward the surrounding changes. The adjustment can only come by developing the flexibility and adaptability from within.

Competency One: Effective Inclusion

The first competency to look at within versatility is inclusion. In leadership and management, the definitions of the two concepts "diversity and inclusion" are regularly used together, and usually diversity before inclusion. From the perspective of a TLC, inclusion is more important than diversity. Inclusion will ensure diversity. Some organizations battle to have a diversity of genders or cultural diversity. Unfortunately, their method of application is wrong. When they apply diversity, they look at the numbers. But there is an important question to ask, for example: "What's the point of including women in leadership if the focus is on the percentage of representation only within the organization and not about providing them the chance to play a bigger role?" It should be about including and engaging women across the organization, not only recruiting women. Same goes for any other types of diversity an organization aims to have.

When we look at how diversity is applied within organizations, we see that it is often all about percentages. Looking more closely at some organizations, we see that diverse members are not well-included within the organization. When we make sure that we are being as inclusive as we can within the organization, including different thoughts, ideas, and voices, this means we are definitely applying diversity. Diversity means listening to input coming from anyone and anywhere within the organization. The mere fact that we are aligned on the meaning of inclusion means, ipso facto, diversity is already being practiced, and various voices are being represented and heard. In that case, inclusion resembles engagement which is one of the most important factors in any organization or society.

One of the most important responsibilities of leaders, within a team context, is to ensure that their team, followers, or those who surround them are engaged with what they are working on, planning, or strategizing, for this is inclusion. Inclusion is about including others as a group or a structure. It's about ensuring that all people, regardless of gender, race, ethnicity, or any other factor, are respected, appreciated, and given a fair chance to be included in all the aspects of the organization. If they don't have inclusion, team members will not be aligned with the vision or the corporate goals; therefore, they will neither be engaged nor motivated and eventually leave.

Inclusion, in this case, means listening with respect and understanding, a high level of empathy, and an open flexible mind that will accept everything that is being raised by the diverse group. Even if leaders reject what is being shared, they need to give it a chance to be discussed by having a flexible mind to look at what's positive, and what adds value to whatever is being shared. For an example, think of the concept of brainstorming, where leaders listen and facilitate discussions, sharing new ideas without any judgment of what is right and wrong at the start. Brainstorming ensures a creativity flux within the organization. Therefore, listening objectively and ensuring that everyone is included is the main factor for creating and facilitating creativity within the organization. By itself, brainstorming is a motivating process for the team, as people feel appreciated and engaged when they are listened to. So, by making sure that they include a diverse group within the organization means they are telling people that leaders are interested in what team members have to offer and they are flexible enough to reach out to them, listen to them, and value their input.

The message that they are sending by being inclusive is so important to the organization's behavior and culture to the extent that it can galvanize the whole energy within the organization. If they're able to apply this mindset across the organization and cascade it down to every level, then every single person becomes a prospective leader.

The essence of inclusion is the intent to include others by listening to what they say and what they don't say. This means that TLCs have to build on what is not being said by opening the space for others to express it.

Sometimes, what is not being said is not intentional; rather, it is being withheld due to not knowing how its expression will fit the system. In such cases, the leaders' responsibility is to notice and open the space for people to explore and express themselves. Once they express their inquiry or observation, TLCs will explore further shared responses to ensure that individuals within the organization are expressing themselves and providing input to the fullest. This is inclusion in its true sense. Inclusion does not mean to ask for peoples' opinions and then set them aside. Inclusion means that, as a leader, I'm interested and I'm curious. With that curiosity comes the power of exploration with inquiry.

If we want to draw an analogy from coaching, coaches sit across from the clients with the commitment to ensure that the clients are the main element within the partnership. Coaches have to continuously look at how to maintain the clients at the center of that relationship. Because there is no hierarchy in coaching, coaches need to include the clients in the relationship by continuously inviting them. Any inquiry or exploration from the coaches is put as an invitation based on respect for and appreciation of the other party. An expression of appreciation means: I'm interested in what you have to say, and I'm keen to explore it with you even if it's not clear to you. I would like to partner together with you so that we can explore it and benefit from what you have to share. This sounds like leaders who have the capacity to embrace coaching as a mindset.

So, intentional listening becomes a reflection of inclusion. Reaching out with courage and flexibility to every individual within an organization to invite them to share what they have on hand is the right application of inclusion. Leaders have to ensure that the team is properly on-boarded and briefed. If they want inclusion to be a centerpiece of the organization, communication is core, whether it be two-way communication or a multi-way communication. Inclusion is not only representation but also visibility: ensuring that every element within the organization is visible, and to be visible they need to be heard.

> *"The essence of inclusion is the intent to include others by listening to what they say and what they don't say. Inclusion means I'm interested and I'm curious."*
>
> — IHAB BADAWI

Competency Two: Uninterrupted Alignment

Once leaders involve the team members in all the aspects of the organization, planning & implementation; once leaders are inviting to listen and share, the doors of alignment and engagement open up. TLCs are aligned internally within themselves, in terms of vision & values, and they make sure to share that alignment with their team.

Why is it important to be aligned, not only within oneself but with the organization and the team as well? It is an invitation for including the team that creates a kind of dialogue. Does that dialogue ensure that everybody understands what is being discussed? Why is it being discussed? Where are they heading with it? And how does it relate to the common goals of the team and organization? Being aligned means that they are on the same page, they are fully informed, they know, they believe, and they support. There is an argument around the degree of alignment and its impact, which asks: does being informed mean that they will support? This is an important question to be answered in a very positive environment that is conducive to having proper dialogue and conversation, where everybody gets the chance to understand why things are being decided this way and where they are heading with such decisions. Even when they have a difference of opinion, that difference is voiced, and when it's voiced and listened to that means it's being appreciated; therefore, resistance will be reduced. This has a very positive impact on the process of change. Therefore, alignment becomes important to facilitate change within the organization and ensures that the way forward becomes smoother.

Among the benefits of alignment are:

- Increased speed in decision-making;
- Better employee engagement;
- Less waste of resources;
- Improved self-governance;
- Less customer confusion;
- Increased respect;
- Resource visibility;
- Optimization of internal talents.

This is all because alignment cannot be achieved without having dialogue, or without informing the team about what they are involved in. Alignment can be best achieved when everyone understands the main objective, understands the higher purpose it serves, and is able to draw the links with their internal values as well.

> *"When leaders embrace coaching, they become vision builders and value shapers."*
>
> — Ihab Badawi

A Vision Builder: Coaches are vision builders in the sense of aligning with the clients and ensuring that the clients are clear on where they want to be: a clear goal, clear objectives, and clear agreement so that they can support the clients moving forward. But the interesting part is that before aligning with that goal, coaches support the clients to maximize the goal so that they can rise to their fullest potential. The same approach is taken by leadership coaches. When engaging with the team, leader-coaches are not engaging them only to inform them about the vision, but to support them to understand it, gain their buy-in around it as it becomes a shared vision, and maximize it through the input of the team.

A Values Shaper: Coaches are value shapers. Coaches support clients to have inner awareness to what they truly believe in, and to be congruent with their values as this will empower them to direct their future. In the same way, TLCs invest the time to facilitate the inner awareness for the team to discover their values and align them with those of the organization. This will ensure that the team is in total alignment internally and externally which will lead to engagement, happiness, and fulfillment. An engaged, happy, and fulfilled team is a high-performance team.

According to Gallup[23], only 27% of employees feel strongly about the values of their organization. Investing in and understanding and actually soliciting feedback from employees increases the feeling of inclusion, creates more well-rounded values around diversity, and builds employee engagement. TLCs build on two-way feedback and actually move toward a feed-forward approach, not only by listening to what people have to say but also by talking with the people and engaging the team based on a future outlook. How do they view the future of the organization? How do they see their role? How do they see their involvement? It's very important to allow team members to have a proper vision of who they will be so that Leader-Coaches can move with them in a more empowering way.

Leader-Coaches can help people create their vision by making them aware of the current & future reality: where they stand and where the organization stands, where they need to head, how they see the future, where they see their role, and how much they want to be part of it. This creates an internal urgency for people to commit and take a step toward what is being discussed. This happens when people are coached by raising their awareness around the common values between them and the organization, and the collective benefit that would result from honoring those common values. If people are coached around what they treasure most, then their relationship with the organization is no longer a financial one only. It becomes a relationship where there is an alignment of principles at a higher level. People will be making the right choices based on the common values and goals of the organization. A starting point for leaders to become TLCs, and until they gain mastery in evoking and shaping values, would be exploring and aligning with their team on the following:

1. Openness to change;
2. Self-enhancement;
3. Conversation; and
4. Self-transcendence.

Competency Three: Resourceful Agility

Agility is an important factor to ensure the proper implementation of versatility. An agile leadership style thrives on removing roadblocks. Being continuously flexible and agile means having a mindset that does not see challenges as a roadblock that stops advancement, but rather see them as an opportunity to make things better. Leaders embracing the agile mindset believe that there is a way, and they just have to identify what's standing in their way and eliminate it. Agility is a representation of flexibility: the capacity to think, act, and connect much faster while being in a mode of acceptance. Acceptance means accepting what's happening and that there is a way out. It has been reported in many organizations that agile teams work better together. Having agile leadership builds and drives agile teams to better business outcomes and results that are achieved with less waste of time and resources. By empowering teams through agility, the organization can unleash the full potential of its human capital. So, why is it important for leaders to embrace agility? It sends a message across the organization, and the team specifically, that there are many ways, not just one way, to look at things, which creates an openness mindset: openness to one another and openness to look at the variables around the team more positively.

Agility empowers the people inside the organization because it facilitates decision-making based on what they already know. It enables them to be resourceful in gathering information and knowledge about what they don't know. In this sense, employees are encouraged to share ideas and to experiment. At its base, agility requires transparent communication. Otherwise, the wealth of information being produced will be lost in the organization. So, TLCs embraces agility to empower other people, and to start preparing the ground for further creativity.

In various interviews and speeches, Jeff Bezos has spoken about the importance of various elements of leaders who embrace agility. The main ones are seven:

1. A customer-centric approach;
2. Focus on the roadmap of the future;
3. Continuous creativity of new businesses or services;
4. Creating multiple ways that will allow a "yes" answer to be on the table;
5. Proper management of big risk;
6. A willingness to take the risk; and
7. Capitalizing on institutional skills.

All the research that I have come across on agile teams focus on three important steps to support them to prosper.

The first is being open, by accepting new ideas and being flexible to change. The second is supporting the team through agile frameworks, methodologies, and tools, using them as a support system, helping the team understand inherited strengths and weaknesses, and setting new goals for building on their strengths and minimizing their development areas so that they can achieve the common goals. The third is shifting the focus from doing agile to being agile. At the core of coaching, the "being" state - to be in the moment, aware of self, and surrounding. The main essence of a coach is to be in the being state, rather than the doing state: being in the moment, being connected to the client, and being able to have awareness of what's happening in the now. A coach embraces an agile mindset, holds no judgment, and flows in a conversation with the client like a river, navigating a path based on the awareness that multiplicity of perspectives exists.

Competency Four: Unrestrained Creativity

Coaches approach clients as being creative and this belief drives the coaches' curiosity. Coaches become curious to know and learn more about the other person, which supports the other person to expand, explore, and be inspired by their learning. Coaches are not trying to prove that they are interesting, they focus all their attention to be interested in the clients. With that curiosity, coaches are able to be creative in posing the right inquiry for the clients, an inquiry that allows the other person to appreciate and take it as an invitation for exploration rather than an interrogation.

It is in the leaders' best interest to embrace the coaching mindset because TLCs look at creativity as a way of life: each day is a new opportunity for new beginnings. TLCs believe that creativity is not their job alone, but that there is a wealth of

THE DOOR TO FLUID LEADERSHIP

innovation and creativity within the organization to tap into. Tapping into that creativity requires the building of an environment that facilitates creative processes, which facilitates sharing and contributing. This helps people to feel empowered in the organization, as they see that the creative environment they are producing is leading to the advancement of the organization and others, giving them a sense of gratification and self-actualization which, in turn, leads to more empowerment.

Organizations or societies which are married to the belief that they can keep repeating what they have been doing and what has worked for them in the past are either rendered obsolete or are on the path to becoming obsolete. The challenge for business leaders in transitioning to become Transcendence Leader-Coaches is that they have been used to linear thinking to implement strategies. Such leaders have not been trained on how to explore radical ideas that will shape the organization or the industry. They have not been used to being in an environment that allows experimentation, failure, and wrong ideas. When they are in a judgmental environment, which either punishes or rewards, there will be no room for a TLC to operate within it. When TLCs facilitate a new thinking process, they allow people to shift their perspective on what they are doing and what they can accomplish.

TLCs come into such an environment and change the whole approach by believing in the team first, trusting the team so that they can trust the process and trust the organization. TLCs are not hungry to provide the answers. They will replace that hunger with curiosity to learn from the team coupled with appreciation and respect. They will spend their time building connections and supporting others to see various connections so that they can see things from different perspectives. TLCs will do what coaches do best: hold a safe space for individuals which allows them to feel secure when they are opening up and exploring new areas.

Creative leaders are like coaches: they see a challenge and jump in to explore what can come from the challenge. Coaches support their clients to embrace that challenge as a new learning path and an opportunity to grow. In this sense, if leaders apply the same approach, leaders will be supporting the team to have the courage to step into unknown territories. Among the creative leaders who have forged new paths in the modern world are Elon Musk, Jack Ma, Bill Gates, Steve Jobs, Walt Disney, and many more.

So, how does it all tie in?

Inclusion is a key to engagement. Leaders can't engage their team if they are not willing to include them in the planning before execution. Including the team is not only beneficial for the team but for the whole organization as it ensures alignment. Alignment on common goals creates focus and opens the door for creativity as people will know how to channel their wisdom and experience. It is said that a confused mind cannot buy, I would add that a confused mind cannot operate and contribute. Thus, alignment is key for creativity. The team will start generating new ideas as leaders appreciate creativity more and more. For creativity to flourish it requires an agile mind, being fluid and flexible to grow and adapt.

Questions to reflect on:

- How flexible am I in dealing with situations?
- How do I accommodate the new ideas of the team?
- When was the last time I accepted a new path other than mine?
- How fast do I accommodate to new thoughts and ideas?
- How inclusive am I?
- What kind of environment did I create to foster creativity?
- How do I promote a culture of inclusion within my team or organization? What specific actions have I taken to ensure that all team members feel valued and included?
- When was a time when I or my team members may have unintentionally excluded someone else? How did I address the situation and work to create a more inclusive environment moving forward?
- How do I ensure that my team members are aligned with the organization's overall goals and vision? What strategies have I found to be effective in promoting alignment and shared understanding among team members?
- How do I typically respond to unexpected or rapidly changing situations in the workplace? When was a time I had to quickly pivot and adapt to a new circumstance?

- ❖ In what ways do I actively seek out new opportunities for growth and development, both for myself and my team? How do I encourage a mindset of continuous learning and improvement?
- ❖ How do I balance the need for structure and planning with the ability to be flexible and adaptable when circumstances require it?
- ❖ When did I make a difficult decision with incomplete information or in a high-pressure situation? How did I approach that decision-making process with agility and resilience?

My Versatility Action Plan

Reflect on your actions and write down in each category 3 actions that will drive you closer to the best version of yourself as a Transcendence Leader-Coach

KEEP DOING	START DOING	STOP DOING

9

SERVICE WITH A SENSE OF PURPOSE

Cluster Three: Service

"A leader is best when people barely know he exists, when his work is done, his aim fulfilled, they will say: we did it ourselves."

— Lao Tzu[24]

THE RISE OF THE TRANSCENDENCE LEADER-COACH

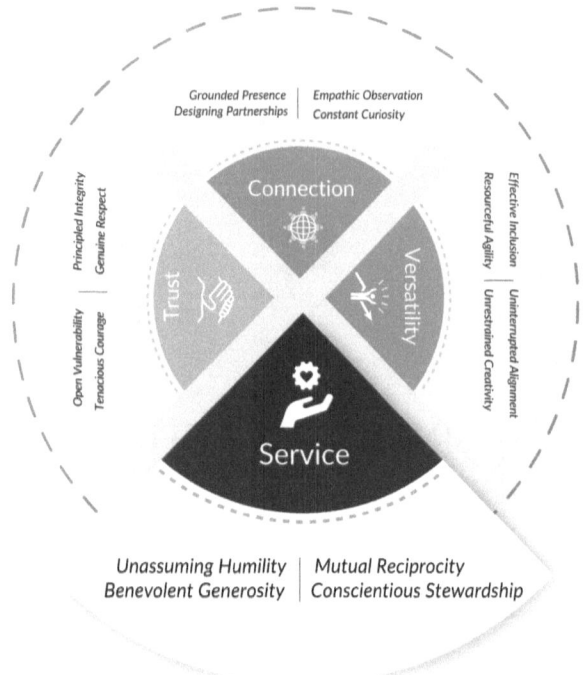

FIGURE 9.1: SERVICE CLUSTER

I spent many years dealing with organizations and managing a few operations in India. On one of my visits to India, I visited a friend in Mumbai who owned a successful garment operation. He used to be rogue, rebellious, and easily triggered. While spending time in his office and then walking around the operation, I started noticing a complete shift in his personality. He was calm, mature, soft-spoken, and above all extremely caring. The best scene I witnessed was seeing my friend helping one of the employees to lift a heavy load and the

SERVICE WITH A SENSE OF PURPOSE

reaction from the employee to that help, a silent joyful appreciation in return for authentic service.

Walking through that vast operation, I was able to feel a new style of leadership that I had not noticed over the seven years I had visited India. It hit me that I had not been looking clearly, with an eye to learn. So, I decided to research the common traits of leaders in India that had shaped my friend for the better. Humility was the secret aspect that created wonders. All successful leaders I looked at had this factor in common. Humility is based on appreciating others no matter what their contribution is, and it is being humble to ensure that differences are not highlighted while operating together. The more humble the leader is, the more accepting the team will be, and the more sense of belonging they will have. Humility, coupled with generosity in relations and conversations before financials, was a point of attraction.

As I spent more time in the operation that I was responsible for in India, I was inspired by seeing a special team-bond form. It was all driven by the head of the operation embracing stewardship. He embraced the common values of the team. Their collective good, rather than an individual agenda, became the drive. This approach was more than enough to let the team contribute strategies that were outside the box and that required a huge effort to execute, and they gladly contributed. All of this was to reciprocate the stewardship of their leader as they saw his focus was on the overall results of the team, rather than his own achievements. Looking closer, I noticed that stewardship was only successful when combined with humility and generosity which yielded the power of reciprocity. The more the leader gave, the more the team was reciprocating in various areas.

The servant leader moves beyond the transactional aspects, and instead actively seeks to develop and align the employee's sense of purpose with the company's mission. This type of leadership requires an individual to demonstrate empathy, listening, and stewardship, which we are going to see in the upcoming competencies. Servant leadership ultimately starts with an unselfish mindset. It's a mindset that focuses on others rather than the self.

If TLCs want to support their team, their main focus becomes removing obstacles from their path. The idea is to serve their growth, interests, and objectives. Leaders embracing coaches' mindset would be able to demonstrate service in its purest sense by focusing on the interests of the team rather than their own interests, understanding who they are, what their true focus and intentions are, and what they aspire to. So, leaders with a service mindset always seek to ensure that interactions move from control toward more synergy and support. Servant leaders create an environment that promotes innovation, empowers employees, focuses on their well-being, and aims to develop others around them. It's important to note that such a mindset is always suitable because, at the end of the day, the main duty of leaders is to support their team and ensure that they can perform at their best, are fulfilled, and are happily motivated.

To ensure that this mentality is embraced and appreciated, servant leaders entice subordinates to serve others as a priority, and as a result, it becomes part of the culture. When everyone tries to serve others, they come across with good intentions, positivity, support, and collaboration. The focus is to share leadership, to share power so that collectively they can win. The main belief for servant leaders is that they can progress and grow through a commitment to serving others, and they reflect the true meaning of leadership, which is not about position.

Leadership is reflected in how they treat others and what values they carry around with them as servant leaders. Servant leadership has lots of good qualities. And the question is, why aren't all leaders embracing such a competency? The answer is that not all leaders are well-educated about the meaning of service and its true impact on others. It takes courage and effort to implement a service mindset and allow such an approach to the surface as it requires a big capacity for change.

Among the areas that servant leaders should act on to provide service is to apply empathetic listening, like coaches listening with no judgment, objectively, and with appreciation and curiosity to understand the other, rather than making themselves understood.

There are four competencies that make up the service cluster: Unassuming Humility, Benevolent Generosity, Conscientious Stewardship, and Mutual Reciprocity.

*"Humility is leading without
the power of authority or hierarchy."*

— IHAB BADAWI

Competency One: Unassuming Humility

Humility is one of the characteristics that are misunderstood in the world. For most, humility is weakness, while humility in the corporate world means leading without the power of authority or hierarchy. Looking at coaching, we start understanding what humility means. In coaching, the relationship does not have a hierarchy, which facilitates the formation of a partnership. When coaches are able to create connections and build partnerships with the team, the team's focus is no longer on following the leader's line of authority, but on being inspired by the leader. The team no longer sees any boundaries.

However, this does not mean that the team will overstep professional boundaries. This requires leaders to apply humility while they are still decision-makers and can inspire the team with the power they can exert in making tough decisions. In such cases, the tough decisions are no longer made to prove status or knowledge, but rather they play a role within the team. Coaches approach the coaching relationship with no hierarchy and with complete humility no matter how experienced they are because humility invites openness to others and connection. When people see knowledgeable and powerful leaders relinquishing power because they prefer to lead by trust, safety, and belief rather than fear of losing their position, people will see the essence of true leadership.

When coaches apply humility in empowering the relationship, there is no pressure for anyone to prove own self. It's not about proving anything: it's about growing together. Any inquiry from the coaches to the clients will then be accepted with an open heart because it's not a clash of egos. Likewise, when leaders embrace humility, they connect with others, start seeing people for who they are, and allow people to see the leaders for who they are. This allows a genuine connection to be created.

Humility is usually associated with other characteristics such as sincerity, modesty, fairness, truthfulness, and authenticity. By combining these characteristics, leaders become more empowered. But, again, a major qualifier is that when we say that servant leaders should have a service mindset, this does not mean that they can be pushed around easily. They have the capacity to stand firm on certain boundaries and are able to have difficult conversations. Humility, in this way, becomes an important attribute, allowing leaders to capitalize on the notion that they should not know everything. This brings a great belief that leaders are more approachable, and therefore it facilitates the steps the team will take to open up because leaders give them a sense of mission. In this sense, humility focuses on the collective good rather than on individualistic goals. Accordingly, leaders become inspired to practice humility by reminding themselves that it's not about showing that they are the best, it's about allowing people to feel their best when they are around the leaders.

Humble leaders will ask for help, and will never claim that they have all the answers. They wear the coaches' hat, where everything is about inquiring and exploring. They'll be the first to admit a mistake and they will never try to shame others about their mistakes. Humble leaders create an open discussion with the team and take responsibility collectively for those mistakes. They will never rely on threats, fear, or intimidation: instead, they display compassion for others, and will always take action to continue their journey of development.

Humility is the basis of generosity, which is the second competency under this group.

Competency Two: Benevolent Generosity

Generosity is the power of giving. When we look at organizations, we see that some leaders and managers misunderstand the concept of giving. They understand giving as being generous with information, support, and time. These are definitely important, but what is more important is the generosity of allowing space for people to share and connect, step up, and have a fair chance to evolve as leaders of the future. For this kind of leader, the TLC generosity is opening the space for others to share that leadership.

SERVICE WITH A SENSE OF PURPOSE

The coach-client relationship provides constant partnering with the client, which is reflected in many areas. One area is empowering the client to choose what happens in the session by exploring and coming up with answers. It is never about coaches giving answers, it is about partnering with clients and exploring what arises with no judgment and no agenda. The relationship is all about exploring what clients want and where they want to go.

Leader-Coaches will reflect generosity by listening and opening the space for clients to talk. Coaches prioritize generosity by being silent, offering space for clients to reflect, rather than talking and affecting the environment. Coaches are generous in many ways, most importantly by maximizing their curiosity for the sake of their clients, not for their own learning.

"The single most important attribute of leadership is generosity."

– Jack Welch[25]

Martin Luther King Jr. once asked, "What are you doing for others?" This question reflects life's most persistent and urgent questions. For leaders to expand with their team, they need to have the belief that it's about the team, not the leaders. The highest form of generosity is not giving money, it is giving their time and focus to others which are more personalized and empowering.

TLCs believe in the abundance of creativity and innovation of others. In the abundance of being a good person, the generosity of TLCs transcends the materialistic aspects and focuses on empowering the team to become leaders on their own. So, to be able to walk, talk, and breathe as generous leaders by elevating to being TLCs, leaders can start by acting on five main areas that will allow others to see that generosity:

1. Allocate time for others. Be accessible and reachable;
2. Share their talent which proves that they are generous when the time comes to transform their skill or knowledge;
3. Embrace truth and honesty by creating a constructive regular feedback process that allows the flow of information across the organization to be fluid; and
4. Give with humanity which means being genuinely concerned and linked to others by giving them the chance to express and act on what they like the most.

> *"Leaders Breed Leaders.*
> *This is the biggest act of generosity."*
>
> — IHAB BADAWI

Competency Three: Conscientious Stewardship

Stewardship is managing the interaction between individuals and placing care at the center. Stewardship leaders are interested in the growth of the organization's mission, vision, and values. The main focus for a steward leader is to attract talents who are aligned, in terms of their individual values with those of the organization. Steward leadership focuses on the collective good and welfare rather than on individual or personal goals. So, leadership cannot manifest itself without maturity, because it takes maturity to be able to transcend beyond one's own interests or career objectives to build healthy and interdependent relationships across the organization. This leaves no room for an individualistic approach. Accordingly, the main component is to align everyone around a shared vision.

John F. Kennedy once said, "Ask not for what the country can offer. Ask not what your country can do for you but what you can do for your country."[26]

In a VUCA world, in times of challenges and crisis, organizations require this type of trait in leaders, who do not think solely of their interests, but think about how they can stick together and form larger bonds that will allow the whole organization to overcome challenges.

Clarify Purpose and Values:

Clearly communicate the organization's mission, vision, and values. Stewardship flourishes when individuals understand the higher purpose and the impact their work has on the larger goal. Aligning personal values with organizational values helps employees feel a stronger connection to their work, fostering a sense of responsibility.

Empower Decision-Making:

Grant individuals the authority and autonomy to make decisions within their roles. Encourage them to take ownership of their responsibilities and find solutions to challenges. When team members feel trusted to make decisions, they are more likely to take initiative and care for the outcomes.

Provide Learning Opportunities:

Offer ongoing training and development opportunities to enhance skills and knowledge. When employees feel that their growth is prioritized, they are more likely to view their roles as long-term commitments. Continuous learning also equips them to make informed decisions that align with the organization's goals.

Promote Open Communication:

Create an environment where open and transparent communication is encouraged. Team members should feel comfortable discussing concerns, sharing ideas, and providing feedback without fear of retribution. Effective communication builds trust and a shared sense of responsibility for the team's success.

Recognize and Reward Stewardship:

Acknowledge and celebrate instances of responsible behavior and exceptional contributions. Publicly recognizing employees who demonstrate stewardship reinforces the importance of these behaviors and sets an example for others. Rewards can range from verbal praise to more tangible incentives, based on the organization's culture and resources.

Enabling stewardship is an ongoing process that requires consistent effort. By following these steps, you can cultivate a culture where individuals take ownership, collaborate effectively, and work towards shared goals with a strong sense of responsibility and care.

Competency Four: Mutual Reciprocity

> *J. W. Marriott famously said: "If you take care of your people, they will take care of your customers and your business will take care of itself."*[27]

Reciprocity is a clear demonstration of how tending to the well-being and optimal growth of individuals profoundly influences their overall welfare. Consequently, teams exhibit dedicated efforts and achieve outcomes with a heightened sense of mindfulness. It's an opportune moment to cultivate patience with each team member and establish interconnectedness within the team fabric.

One of the notably effective strategies employed by adept leaders in their coaching endeavors is the deliberate allocation of time for both one-on-one and group coaching sessions, beyond the realm of operational concerns. Leaders invest in caring for and engaging with their teams as an integral facet of the coaching process. These interactions transcend mere work-related discussions and extend to the exploration of personal objectives, aspirations, preferences, and alignment with the organization's overarching vision. This approach highlights that leaders prioritize not only organizational objectives but also the team members as individuals.

As a result, the teams unanimously report a heightened sense of being nurtured and a deepened sense of belonging. This approach solidifies the notion that leaders are genuinely invested in the holistic growth of their teams, fostering an environment where each individual's well-being is not only acknowledged but actively nurtured.

Reciprocity can be very effective when applied in an honest, meaningful, and ethical manner. It is crucial to have a leader-coach mindset in offering real value to the team. When showing appreciation for others, the whole relationship is humanized and team members will start valuing the leader. The team will search for the means to give back to the organization and the leader at the same time.

> *"Give before you receive and you will command loyalty."*
>
> – NAPOLEON HILL[28]

How does it all tie in?

Look at the components of steward leadership. Stewardship in organizations shares lots of analogies with coaching. The whole concept of stewardship in business is centered around personal vision, personal mastery, vulnerability, valuing diversity, experimentation, risk-taking, raising awareness, and delivering results. From each of these elements, we can draw analogies with and learn lessons from coaching, which is why leaders should embrace coaching. When it comes to personal vision, coaches support clients to have a clear personal vision that drives them to achieve. That personal vision becomes the compass that leaders can use to empower their team by allowing them to understand their vision as it aligns with that of the organization. At that point, the vision becomes a shared one. Coaches support clients to explore and expand their inner potential so that clients gain mastery in taking hold of their own potential and directing it toward their own objectives.

Raising awareness is at the heart of coaching. Coaching is all about deepening the learning and heightening the awareness for the client. Delivering results naturally evolves from the coaching process, where coaches support clients to outline their results, draft the right action plan, and support them in determining the best course of action.

When leaders embrace coaching, they are able to apply all of these components. When leaders apply all of these competencies, not only from an individual perspective, but from the team, organizational, and social perspective, stewardship becomes embedded in the leaders' approach. The TLC focuses on supporting the team to have a complete awareness of who they are, what their vision is, what their potential is, and how they can take full command of their potential while aligning around common goals which are embedded in the shared vision. Trust becomes a guiding factor, whereby all the team members of the organization reach out to each other without holding back, without being afraid of being judged. They are honest, authentic, and transparent in seeking help and diving into experimenting with new choices as they believe they are in a judgment-free, safe environment. This will enable them to raise their awareness and have better clarity about their actions and the results they seek.

Questions to reflect on:

- ❖ How do I serve others?
- ❖ When I serve others, do I do it so that they notice what I have done?

SERVICE WITH A SENSE OF PURPOSE

- ❖ When was the last time I served someone at a great cost to myself without keeping track of the cost?
- ❖ Are there people in my life that I am resisting serving due to selfishness?
- ❖ Are there people I avoid serving in order to help others that will give me something in return?
- ❖ What really motivates me to serve others?
- ❖ Am I serving others wholeheartedly?
- ❖ Do I complain in my heart or to those closest to me after I have served at great cost? What is the impact of my complaints?
- ❖ Do I seek out ways in which to serve others joyfully? How?

THE RISE OF THE TRANSCENDENCE LEADER-COACH

My Service Action Plan

Reflect on your actions and write down in each category 3 actions that will drive you closer to the best version of yourself as a Transcendence Leader-Coach.

KEEP DOING	START DOING	STOP DOING

10

TRUST IS EVERYTHING

Trust Is the Key to Open & Authentic Conversations

Cluster Four: TRUST

"Without trust we don't truly collaborate, we merely coordinate or, at best, cooperate. It is trust that transforms a group of people into a team."

— Stephen Covey[29]

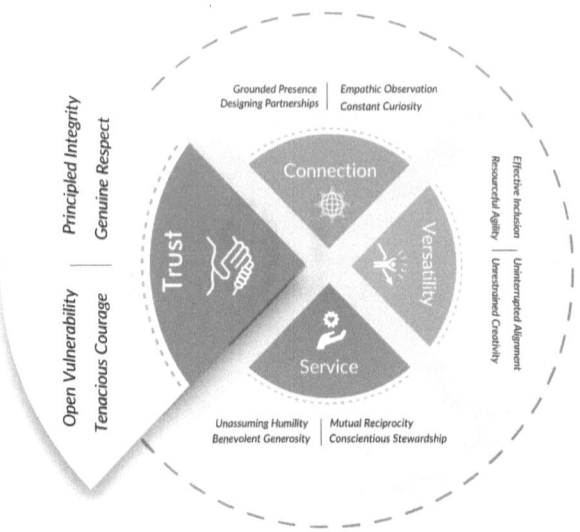

FIGURE 10.1: TRUST CLUSTER

To understand trust, we have to look at the impact of distrust. While walking once in a hallway with a coaching client, a member of the cost accounting team approached my client, a newly assigned Managing Director, to share some information. The employee seemed worried and requested permission to talk in private. The MD gave him permission to speak in front of me. So, the employee shared the disturbing news. The employee identified certain discrepancies that reflected a high level of waste which might be linked to possible unethical practices at the production site. The immediate reaction from the MD was to reject the findings and react in a very harsh manner in the face of an employee who meant well. The MD did not trust any interpretation except his own. The MD walked away, leaving the employee standing in the hallway. The employee turned to me and said, "No matter what I find out from now on, I would never report beyond my responsibility. If he does not trust what I say, then why should I bother?"

I spent a few minutes talking to the employee about the duties of an ethical employee until he calmed down. However, the harm was already done with a deep impact, not to the employee alone but to the whole organization. Later, I learned that the reactions of the MD based on his lack of trust and his belief that he knew it all, had a 9% impact on the company's waste factor. Working with the MD on a few coaching sessions, the MD started discovering the opportunity lost by not trusting the team members. His lack of respect and appreciation contributed to a culture of disengagement. Learning to be vulnerable, a concept that he had interpreted as weakness, had a profound impact on him and his team. By discovering how to let go of his "I know it all" and "I control it all" mindset, the MD understood the true power of vulnerability. He started opening up to the team and requesting support from their experience and input. He saw first-hand that his actions were interpreted as an act of courage and trust toward the team members. This is usually the case when such actions are based on integrity. The MD was genuine with his transformation and was shocked to see the improvements in a relatively short period as people always prefer a culture of trust to grow and prosper.

THE RISE OF THE TRANSCENDENCE LEADER-COACH

Effective leadership requires lots of skills, competencies, and capabilities, so trust becomes the binding factor. The neuroscience of trust appeared in a 2017 *Harvard Business Review* article by Professor Paul Zak[30] who wrote that, compared to people at low-trust companies, people at high-trust companies report less stress, 6% more energy at work, 50% higher productivity, 13% less sick days, 76% more engagement, 29% more satisfaction with their lives, and 40% less burnout. By looking at these numbers we can see how trust contributes to the welfare of the organization.

It's also reported and a well-known fact that when people feel that they are taken care of or feel that they are operating in a positive environment, their productivity increases.

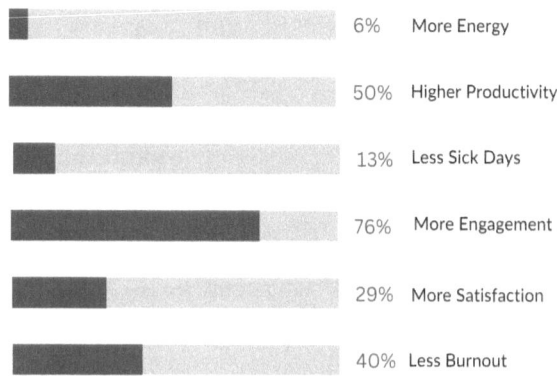

FIGURE 10.2: TRUST CONTRIBUTION INDEX

The most trusted leaders in the organization are those who inspire and encourage greatness, integrity, teamwork, and resilience. These factors are important to developing and maintaining trust, between the leader, the team, and the organization. The most influential factors to promoting these components is building capability, honesty, and authenticity. A good leader will trust others, but also know when and how to shape that trust into reality. Blind trust leads to blind spots, and therefore trust has to be implemented along with other competencies. Again, if leaders want to embed and build on trust within their leadership approach, the fastest route is to embrace coaching which is all about trust. Without trust, there is no partnership with clients, which is essential in moving forward. Without trust, clients will not open up and will not feel safe to explore.

TLCs communicate with positivity and in an empowering tone, based on trusting their team's potential and capability, and that trust creates motivation and empowerment. To build and strengthen trust within the organization, 5 things have to exist all of which are encompassed in coaching:

1. Skill Development;
2. Empowerment;
3. Transparency;
4. Communication; and
5. Character development.

In this cluster, we have four competencies: Open Vulnerability, Tenacious Courage, Principled Integrity, and Genuine Respect.

Competency One: Open Vulnerability

> *"Admitting one's mistake is a testament to one's courage. It is through this act of vulnerability that true power is revealed."*
>
> – Ihab Badawi

To drop our armor that protects us from feeling vulnerable, and to be able to lower our emotional shields requires opening up, stepping up, and reaching out to others. One of the signs of vulnerability is knowing what's wrong, admitting that we are wrong, and not being afraid of being judged on who we are and what our position is. For leaders to step up and admit that they are wrong reflects power and contributes to building relationships that are based on trust and transparency. When leaders dare to admit that they are wrong, the team feels safe and becomes honest about what is at stake. They will not be afraid of being judged and will reach out to leaders or other team members for support in the same way leaders stepped up and admitted their mistakes.

> *"Vulnerability is not weakness. And that myth is profoundly dangerous. Vulnerability is the birthplace of innovation, creativity, and change."*
>
> – Brene Brown[31]

Dr. Brene Brown has done a lot of research on vulnerability, and in her book *The Power of Vulnerability*[32] concluded that vulnerability is engaging in life, being all in, and dedicating yourself to something. Leaders who can express vulnerability are people who do not feel that they should be the first to answer or to come up with all the ideas. Vulnerable leaders, especially in a VUCA world, will have a different mindset, a mindset that believes that reaching out to others and seeing through their eyes is more empowering. Such leaders have the willpower to reach out to different members, peers, or team members in the organization for support, which becomes an invitation for conversations that will drive and lead to change. It will lead people to become more invested in what leaders have to share. Being vulnerable is not only about being open about mistakes, but also being open to admitting not knowing something, and willing to reach out to others for support.

Most managers think that by answering all the questions they show ownership, confidence, and knowledge; they show power which is what will drive, strengthen, and fortify their leadership, and this is where all goes wrong. Leadership does not have to be exerted on people; on the contrary, it is earned. Leaders need to earn the trust of people because one cannot influence others by pushing them away. They need to train the vulnerability muscle by actually practicing it.

Vulnerability is not only about admitting mistakes. For example, when leaders say to someone, "I was wrong about you," imagine how this message is received. It shows full transparency and full courage; therefore, the other person feels appreciated and encouraged to speak freely, respecting the leaders' action which displays their vulnerability.

When we look at the coaching relationship, we notice that coaches embrace vulnerability because, without vulnerability, coaches tend to make the mistake of being judgmental or trying to show that they are professionals who know it all. In doing so, they might step into the story of the clients, and this will have a damaging effect on the coaching relationship. They enter the relationship with the mindset that "it's okay for me not to know and I'm not supposed to know the client's story or all the client's needs." It's okay to ask a question that they don't know the answer for. It is okay to take responsibility for this partnership and invite clients into it because it's an exploration based on trust. They don't need to know every step to start exploring. Coaches express vulnerability by being curious about areas that might be completely unknown.

Calmness, rather than emotional outbursts, bring maturity. For Dr. Brene Brown, one of the main barriers for us is our fear of losing connection with others, and therefore, it is the biggest fear because we believe that if we disconnect, shame will produce fear which will then stop us and discourage us from getting vulnerable. Expressing vulnerability empowers kinships, and therefore it allows us to face uncertainty, risk, and emotional exposure. It can create space for productive failure, where we all learn from failures. Dr. Brown suggests that leaders should create a culture where discomfort is synonymous with moving in the right direction because it means we are all growing more productively.

Among the benefits of vulnerability is, first, establishing meaningful & genuine connections to reflect trust. Even though it sometimes makes leaders feel uncomfortable, vulnerability yields greater connections with others because it is genuine.

The second benefit is greater innovation because vulnerability allows leaders to lead with a mind that fosters creativity. It establishes an environment of safety, and when there is safety, people are no longer held back from thinking differently or contributing because of the risks.

The third benefit of vulnerability is expanding the scope of help and accepting the help of others by reaching out to the team. It sends a message that it's okay to seek help, and therefore, the team becomes more empowered by one another. Operating on a shared responsibility reduces the risk on each individual and reduced risk means reduced anxiety.

Competency Two: Tenacious Courage

It also takes courage to be empathetic, listen without judgment, and isolate one's experience. Focusing on the other person, and showing appreciation for what they know without comparing it to what we know takes courage. It translates into compassion to notice what others are passing through with a desire to alleviate it. Courage comes from the Latin word *core* meaning heart, to tell the story of who we are with our whole heart. When we are compassionate with ourselves, it invites us to turn it outwards to be compassionate with others.

Courageous leaders lead others by fostering confidence, and that confidence is reflected in every move. Confidence is shown by having an open mind, being without expectation, having a belief based on positivity and abundance, and believing that there are lots of opportunities for them out there. They have the courage to reach out to those opportunities because courage is a muscle that they have strengthened through the choices they have made. It is through courage that they make the decisions that will lead them to taking action that can stretch their capability; therefore, courage becomes a key aspect of facilitating growth.

Authentic leaders start by having the courage to look in the mirror and see what they stand for: what strengths they have, what areas they have to develop, and what they need to work on. Having the courage to say, "I need to develop in this area or I need to tame myself" builds self-discipline by exerting control and reflecting a higher executive presence within the organization.

Competency Three: Principled Integrity

Integrity, as a competency, is an essential component of organizational life, society, and our daily lives. One of the keys to a positive and productive work environment is having leaders who act with integrity. Integrity, in this sense, reflects honesty, trustworthiness, and reliability. Integrity is important for a positive and productive environment because it is a universal value that everyone connects to, and when we integrate it as a competence, as something that we build our actions and behavior around, we can build trust with everyone around us.

Integrity, in the sense of being honest, means speaking one's mind and having the courage to admit mistakes, express opinions freely, and share input while respecting the organizational environment. To gain a better perspective and understanding of one's own integrity, ask: As a leader, am I being accountable for my behavior? Am I acting with responsibility for the decisions that I'm making? Am I following through with my commitments? Am I leading by example? Do I abide, as a leader, by what I preach within the organization? All of these are aspects of building integrity internally in the organization. Each individual question builds credibility. So, in essence, to have integrity in the organization and build on this competency means that we build credibility across the organization starting with our team, our peers, and the leadership team.

Coaches build on their integrity and embrace it in every aspect of their professional life by the way they communicate with clients even before they become their clients. Because their message is authentic, professional coaches abide by what they advocate because creating impact for the clients is based on the coaches' ability to act as a mirror. Coaches reflect the clients with no distortions, without leading them, and mirror the clients to allow them to understand reality and listen to what they have said with no additions. For coaches to be able to reflect, integrity has to be integrated within their empathetic listening. So, start with applying empathetic listening by asking yourself: Am I making sure that I'm listening objectively without analyzing others and not involving my story within their story? Am I deducing, generalizing, or drawing conclusions?

To have a sense of integrity within the organization, TLCs should be fair witnesses. This means being honest and transparent in every interaction with everyone and providing transparent messaging across the organization without any emotional attachment. It's very important to always check-in and assess themselves as leaders: When I'm listening, what's my intention? Am I listening to understand or listening to respond? Am I listening to appreciate or am I waiting for my chance to respond with what I know? Am I being objective with the questions or are my questions emotionally charged or heading into areas that I want to go into as a leader? From time to time, the TLCs take a step back and reflect on how they are, their strengths, weaknesses, successes, and failures as if they are looking at themselves from the outside. An important question to ask so that they can apply this step as TLCs is, "What would others say about the way I am showing up?" and be ready to answer with full integrity.

It is said that no matter how intuitive, persuasive, and resourceful leaders are, if those leaders lack integrity, then they are ultimately bound to fail.

"If there is no respect, there is no trust."

— ANONYMOUS

Competency Four: Genuine Respect

As the main competency under this cluster, it's important to see how respect is earned and not forced on others. It is a reward for how leaders show up and how they manifest their leadership approach within an organization, as a team, and with others. There are two ways to lead people: either through fear or through respect. Leading people through fear might push them to perform and finalize tasks on time. However, at some point, the relationship between the team and the leader will break because the relationship will become transactional. People who fear their leader or their organization will establish a mindset where they see their relationship with the organization as that of doing work and getting paid for it. There is no space for happiness in the work environment where there is fear. Therefore, the level of engagement within the organization reduces.

The maximum level of job satisfaction that can be seen in such an environment is getting paid enough for the hours being worked. However, with a prolonged level of fear that satisfaction itself drops as well, and at some point, the relationship will break because fear will yield anxiety, and people who operate under anxiety and stress are prone to make mistakes. Making mistakes will cause them to fear even more, so it becomes a cycle and they will be held accountable. Once this happens, they often either decide to leave or are asked to leave. In the long run, leading through fear is counterproductive. Unfortunately, some managers see the immediate payback of leading with fear, as it pleases their ego; therefore, they accept it as mainstream.

Leading with respect, on the other hand, has long-term, sustainable impact within the organization. Respecting other people's ideas and respecting them as human beings amplifies all other aspects within the organization starting with listening. This in turn makes people feel appreciated, and a sense of gratitude starts to become established. When leaders talk to people with respect, they are expressing their point of view while respecting theirs. This shows that they are open and accepting of what they have to offer, not necessarily to build on it and move on, but as a sign of inclusion within the organization. Therefore, it draws in their team members rather than drawing them out. There's a high sense of reciprocity when it comes to respecting. If they respect others, with time, that respect is reciprocated.

This is how respect cascades through the organization. If leaders are providing feedback while respecting other people's emotions, reactions, and personalities, people will become more open to accepting feedback and they become better listeners. Respect by itself causes good connections to become established within the organization.

Respect in coaching is extremely important. Part of establishing trust and safety in the relationship between a coach and a client is respecting the client's input, thoughts, values, beliefs, perspectives, and contributions within the session. Even if clients are not making any headway in the session, coaches respect their intent in their commitment to showing up for the sessions and making an effort to move forward. Coaches anchor respect in their mindset even before starting the session, which means coaches say, "I will respect my client's time, presence, and wholeness in the session."

This includes respecting the clients' space and what they are capable of, even though they may not have achieved a breakthrough yet. Respect supports the "yet" aspect, the belief that things will happen but have not happened yet. This in itself empowers the relationship between coaches and clients. Professional coaches do not fake respect: they believe in it, act on it, and practice it, and it becomes integral in the way they show up with clients. There is no effort to be made, there is nothing to act on. It is already embedded in the process of coaching and the presence of coaches with clients. Respect empowers active and empathetic listening because when coaches respect the speaker that means they are listening without judgment, without analysis. This is why we say that leaders should embrace the TLC approach because they will anchor respect as one of their core competencies, treating it as a way of life, a way of communication.

There are many ways for leaders to reflect respect within the organization, and once it becomes a mode of behavior, leaders will respect every single component of the organization. The organization becomes not about hierarchy, but about dealing and respecting fellow team members. This becomes extremely empowering for the team and the organization as a whole.

> *"Respect is contagious."*
>
> – IHAB BADAWI

When leaders exhibit genuine respect for their team, this sentiment reverberates throughout the entire organization, as individuals tend to emulate the behavior they witness. The foundation for this transformative dynamic lies in the role of the Transcendence Leader-Coach, who begins by extending respect towards the very principles and values they hold in high regard.

This journey commences with a commitment to alignment between words and actions—a commitment that demonstrates integrity and reinforces the team's trust in their leader. By adhering to organizational norms, rules, and cultural tenets, the Transcendence Leader-Coaches set a compelling example that resonates across the workforce. Their willingness to acknowledge their own fallibility demonstrates humility and further deepens the connections of trust with their team.

Moreover, the Transcendence Leader-Coach actively embraces feedback, recognizing its potential to improve both personal and organizational effectiveness. This willingness to consider diverse viewpoints underscores their openness to growth and their understanding that organizational progress thrives on the collective contributions of all members.

In essence, the leader's respect becomes a transformative force that nurtures a culture of mutual regard and accountability. This cascading effect, driven by the authentic and principled actions of the Transcendence Leader-Coach, fosters an environment where respect is reciprocal, communication is transparent, and collaboration flourishes.

The TLCs will make sure to share their appreciation of others in public and leave any developmental feedback to be shared one-to-one. They ensure that any difference in opinion can be shared and discussed while always regarding others' opinions. This allows mature conversations to manifest across the organization. TLCs ensure an understanding of the environment the company operates within, and understand the people so that they can respect their differences to uphold diversity within the organization. As mentioned earlier, when diversity is coupled with inclusion, creativity within the organization increases. To ensure that they are respecting others, they also have to ensure that they are acting in fairness to all involved, making sure that they're sending the right message as everyone will look to how they are applying standards across the organization. As long as there is no bias, people become more accepting as they feel that their sense of pride and fairness has been valued.

There are steps that leaders can take to ensure that respect is embedded while transitioning to becoming TLCs:

1. Leading by example; Walking the talk;
2. Welcoming two-way communication, new opinions, ideas, and feedback;
3. Being conscious of the choice of words and the place of words. Gaining maturity in realizing what to say and when to say it is another way to show respect;
4. Merging empathetic listening with curiosity. This is done by engaging in a conversation with an intention to learn rather than to prove a point; and
5. Being attentive by listening to what is said and what is not said. Being attentive connects them to the multi-dimensional environment around them.

Questions to reflect on:

❖ How frequently do I honor agreements?
❖ How often do I share information willingly?

- How frequently do I admit mistakes?
- What do I do to maintain trust with those around me?
- How much do I honor openness?
- Who is the person I trust the most? What are his or her characteristics?
- How do I communicate trust?
- What are some examples of trust I have seen in different areas of my work or life?
- What are some things that are going well with trust in my group?
- As I listen to others talk about what has gone well and what has been difficult, what are some themes I am hearing? What is insightful about these themes?
- How will I know that I can trust the future of my organization and my leaders as I move forward?
- What keeps trust going even when times are tough?
- What are some specific actions I can take in the short term to create thriving, sustainable, organizational and individual trust in the future?

THE RISE OF THE TRANSCENDENCE LEADER-COACH

My Trust Action Plan

Reflect on your actions and write down in each category 3 actions that will drive you closer to the best version of yourself as a Transcendence Leader-Coach.

11

WHERE DOES TRUE LEADERSHIP START?

The 3 Keys to Becoming a Transcendence Leader-Coach

*"Unless you change how you are,
you will always have what you've got."*

– JIM ROHN

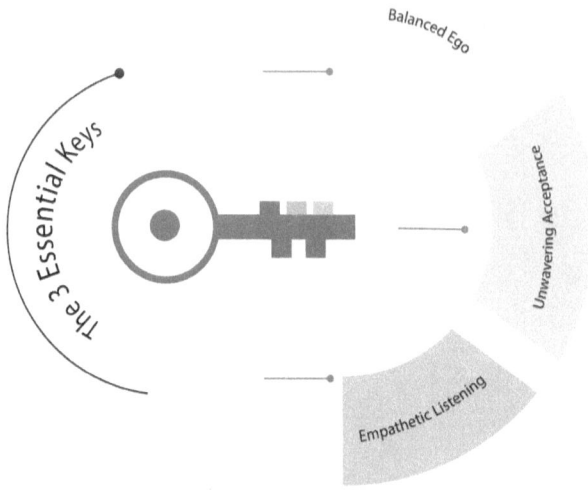

FIGURE 11.1: THE 3 KEYS

How can a leader transcend to become a Transcendence Leader-Coach? Where to begin?

There is no doubt that becoming a Transcendence Leader-Coach starts by working on your mindset and focusing on how to embrace the Six Pillars and embed them in the way you work, talk, and engage others until they become part of you, part of your belief.

The 3 keys to unlocking the TLC framework are:

WHERE DOES TRUE LEADERSHIP START?

1. The First Key – A Balanced Ego

Managing your ego is an essential step. It is said that there are three in a coaching relationship: the coach, the client, and the client's ego. A coach is able to build a relationship with the client based on trust and safety so that the ego is set aside and the coach can transcend with the client beyond their ego. Doing so, a TLC tries to acquire multi-dimensional awareness and will start looking internally to see if own ego is in check. A TLC asks: Am I able to self-manage? Do I understand myself well? How do I know where I stand? What makes me tick? How is my state impacting the session and my client? What is the impact that I create in the world?

Ego management, therefore, starts with leaders taking an inner journey that allows them to discover their core values, belief system, and how it has guided their actions and decisions throughout the years. They have a clear vision as to what type of leader and person they would like to show up as because having that clear vision is the guiding force to move forward. It acts as an internal motivation for leaders to transcend to a higher place, to become a better version of themselves, which is manifested through their leadership approach.

To master this first key, TLCs must master emotional intelligence in its purest form, mastering the capability to understand oneself truly with full transparency, with no intention to be in denial or to hide. They need to open up, be vulnerable and clear toward themselves about how they want to show up with that awareness to manage every element that guides their actions. Managing those elements means balancing their values, clearing out their belief system, setting the right intention internally, and selecting the environment they would like to be in: the organization and the team, finding links between themselves and the environment so that they can be totally aligned. In doing so they will create an environment that supports their ability to manage their ego.

> *"An unchecked ego has a destructive force that leads any leader to operate opposite to the TLC Framework."*
>
> – Ihab Badawi

Our ego can put us in a state where we can't admit mistakes, and it, therefore, goes against the concepts of vulnerability, honesty, integrity, respect, openness, flexibility, and growth. Our ego may stop us from being honest with ourselves to improve. In some cases, the ego will act on us by resembling fear which is opposite to what we are advocating as a TLC: to have the courage to speak up without fearing that one's ego might be hurt.

> *"Leaders don't manage people, they manage energy."*
>
> – Anonymous

The ego represents a major drive within leaders, and if they're able to manage it, it can allow them to move toward great results.

WHERE DOES TRUE LEADERSHIP START?

To keep their ego in check, they have to always remember that it's not about them: it's about the people they work with. So, it's very important not to mix ego with self-esteem or self-importance because leaders are supposed to have a level of confidence to inspire others which come from self-esteem, from how they see their worth. They can maintain high self-esteem and high self-confidence without letting their ego blind them. When the ego gets out of hand it backfires on them as leaders, putting them in a position of not seeing they are wrong, while others can see and do notice that they are wrong. The ego affects their ability to listen and becomes a filter where they start to hear feedback as accusations. One important technique to keep their ego in check is to ask quality questions, and this is why coaching is effective in working with clients without harming their egos. By asking good questions, they will be breaking that cycle. Questions can be:

- What do you know for sure?
- How is this serving you?
- What seems not to be working for you?
- What's standing in your way?
- What needs to shift so you can change the situation?
- How can you shift the situation so that it can add value?

The steps you can take to keep your ego in check are:

1. First, attain self-awareness and understand where your ego stands;
2. Second, leave your ego at the door when you enter into a conversation with others or during a meeting. Park the

emotional aspect aside and focus on your intention because intention drives the way you speak, act, and behave;
3. Third, do not compare yourself with others. While many people resist the temptation to compare themselves with others, sometimes comparing makes you feel better, makes you feel more important and this becomes a negative habit. So, refrain from comparisons. The best comparison that TLCs can make is to compare themselves with their future self. They have a clear picture of who they want to be, how they want to show up, then keep benchmarking with that image until they reach and maintain it;
4. Fourth, connect to a higher purpose. TLCs make sure to remember what impact they would like to create in this world, and that impact becomes a driving force;
5. Fifth, embrace an attitude of service, remembering that supporting others keeps your ego in check;
6. Sixth, continue evolving and learning because every time you learn something new, you are reminded that you don't know everything.

2. The Second Key – Unwavering Acceptance

The second key is acceptance. Acceptance is not being passive, or being in a mode of inaction. In the coaching process coaches need to accept what is and accept what can be. Accepting "what is" means accepting the current reality, that it exists for a reason, that they can learn from it and that there is something ahead.

Accepting "what can be" is accepting the concept of abundance and hope, which finds opportunities in adversity.

> *"Acceptance, in reality, is the opposite of indifference."*
>
> – IHAB BADAWI

By accepting the reality of a situation, leaders take action with total empowerment, not resisting the situation, but receiving it courageously with open arms. They are not receiving it to adapt to it, but to evolve with it in the direction of their vision and where they want to be. It starts by accepting themselves as they are. It all comes back to self-awareness. That's why we say leadership starts by understanding the self, and with self-awareness, when we achieve self-leadership, then we can lead others. Acceptance extends to accepting others' views and respecting their input, ideas, and presence. Leaders accept them as valuable individuals and unique human beings. This will unlock many factors for them in terms of establishing trust, respect, safety, and humility. Lack of acceptance leads to mistrust, and mistrust leads to negativity which leads to anxiety. This is the opposite of what the TLC stands for.

3. The Third Key – Empathetic Listening

Listening is the third key. Listening empathetically with no judgment or analysis is key: listening to understand rather than being understood. Coaches Listen because they are interested in the other person and not preoccupied in looking interesting for others. In that way, listening goes beyond merely hearing others, being quiet, or just paying attention. It requires that they are present in the moment, connected, aware of what is said and what is not being said, and understanding the context within which others speak.

If listening were a job, then it would be a 24-hour job for leaders. For Peter Drucker[33]*, the most important thing in communication is hearing what isn't said because, when you unlock your intuition as a Leader-Coach, your listening is amplified: you start to listen to what is not being said. By sensing the environment and the person in front of them and then adding to that the curiosity to ask and inquire, leaders eliminate judgment from the interaction which will enable them to know that their sense is correct. Asking questions objectively opens the door for empathetic listening to be enhanced. The quality of their listening affects the quality of the information they take in and therefore the perceptions they have. People want to be heard and respected, but they want to be understood and felt as well. Listening provides that respect and understanding as long as they are listening without filters. Coaches listen 80% of their time, which reflects how much they respect their clients.

> *Andy Stanley says, "Leaders who do not listen will eventually be surrounded by people who have nothing to say."*[34]

WHERE DOES TRUE LEADERSHIP START?

This quote is quite profound because when leaders continue to talk, others will step back and not want to share. Eventually, the environment falls into silence, and they deprive themselves of valuable input, opportunities for growth, and information that can support them to face the challenges of the VUCA world. So, my invitation to you is to use the 3 keys and unlock your internal awareness so you can transform your mindset and transcend your leadership approach to become a Transcendence Leader-Coach – TLC.

Questions to reflect on:

- How humble am I?
- How objective is my listening?
- What proof do I have that I listen objectively?
- What am I doing to improve my listening?
- How do I deal with changes?
- How do I define success, and how does that definition relate to my ego?
- How do I react to criticism or negative feedback? Is there a pattern in how I respond to it?
- Can I think of a time when my ego may have interfered with a decision or action I took? How did I handle it, and what would I do differently now?
- How do I empower my team to make decisions, and how do I balance that with my own desire for control or recognition?
- What steps do I take to ensure that my ego does not overshadow the needs of the team or the organization as a whole? How do I hold myself accountable for this?

My Keys Action Plan

Reflect on your actions and write down in each category 3 actions that will drive you closer to the best version of yourself as a Transcendence Leader-Coach.

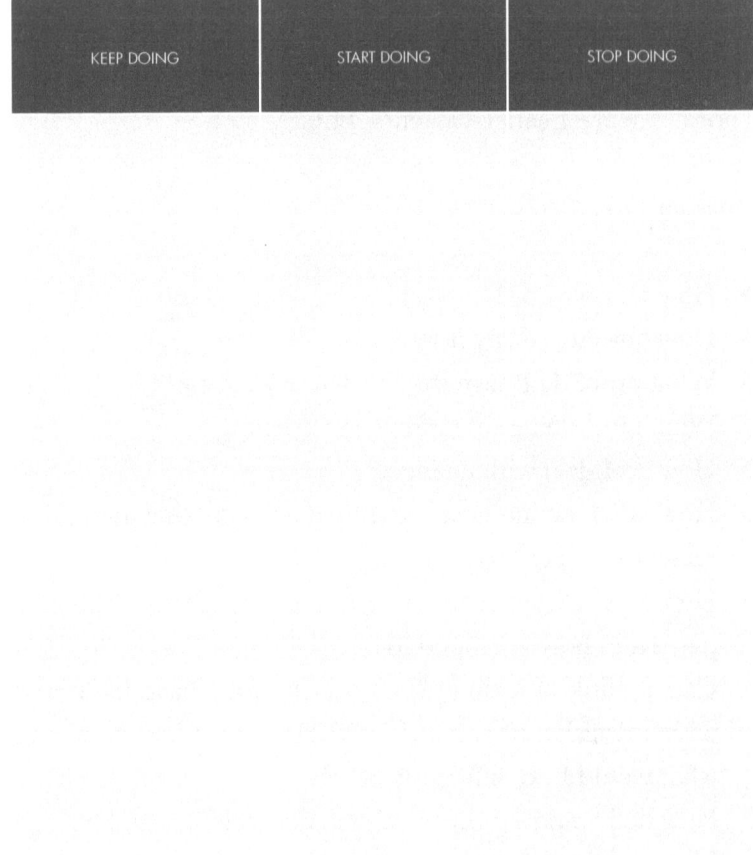

Conclusion

You have now finished reading this book and you are reflecting on which areas you need to adopt. You're probably wondering, where do I begin?

I suggest you start by looking again at the notes you have taken at the end of each chapter (or at the mental notes you have made on each chapter) and start reflecting on the best plan of action for you to move toward becoming a Transcendence Leader-Coach, or to develop new Transcendence Leader-Coaches within your organization.

The intention of this book is to provide you with a reflective space to reconsider your leadership approach in relation to what is truly needed in your organization to navigate the dynamic complexities surrounding you. It is intended to help create a human-centric leadership environment around you by embracing the Transcendence Leader-Coach Framework: the 6 mindset pillars and the 16 core competencies.

The Six Pillars:

1. Gratitude;
2. Bliss;
3. Abundance;
4. Positivity;
5. Growth; and
6. Forward-thinking.

The Sixteen Competencies:

a. Connection
    i. Grounded Presence
    ii. Empathetic Observation
    iii. Constant Curiosity
    iv. Designing Partnership
b. Versatility
    i. Effective Inclusion
    ii. Uninterrupted Alignment
    iii. Resourceful Agility
    iv. Unrestrained Creativity
c. Service
    i. Unassuming Humility
    ii. Benevolent Generosity
    iii. Conscientious Stewardship
    iv. Mutual Reciprocity

d. Trust
   i. Open Vulnerability
   ii. Tenacious Courage
   iii. Principled Integrity
   iv. Genuine Respect

If you have any questions about how to go about implementing the TLC framework, you can either refer to my contact details in my biography and I will gladly attend to your inquiry, or you can listen to my podcast or subscribe to my newsletter on my website so you can be invited to regular MasterClasses during which we share our teachings around the framework.

Some More Offerings

To support you further, I would like to offer you further resources that would support you in your journey to becoming the next Transcendence Leader-Coach. You can now join me for free on the following channels:

- ❖ podcast
- ❖ Blog
- ❖ Masterclasses

Subscribe through my website:

www.ihabbadawi.com

Author's Biography

Ihab is an international catalyst for change who supports individuals and organizations to re-envision their leadership approach by embracing the power of coaching. Being inspired by the power of coaching, he has dedicated the past 15 years to creating a positive impact for both individuals and organizations by instilling a new paradigm that leads to embracing coaching as a culture. Driven by his passion, he has developed a unique coaching model: "Transcendence Coaching - The DNA of Coaching," which is now being taught to certify international coaches by The Coaches Circle Academy. Ihab founded The Coaches Circle Academy to impact millions by developing internationally certified professional coaches and by supporting organizations to create a new breed of leaders who embrace coaching as a culture.

Ihab is also the founder of Interactive Business Gears (IBG), a firm that specializes in organizational leadership through human capital optimization. He is a Corporate

Advisor & Leadership Coach with over 22 years of experience in International Business Management, Corporate Transformation, and International Business Development. He spearheaded operations across 58 countries around the globe while holding various leading roles as Chief Commercial Officer, Vice President, and Managing Director for leading organizations in the MEA region, the Indian Subcontinent, ASEAN, and China.

During his corporate journey, Ihab has led major culture reengineering projects and rebuilt leadership teams across various operations, leading to successful transformations in organizational behavior and building high-performance cultures. His cross-cultural exposure has contributed to his capability to research and embrace various leadership traits that has led him to craft the Transcendence Leader-Coach Framework.

Currently, Ihab advocates the Transcendence Leader-Coach Framework across various organizations and supports in developing leaders capable of embracing this new leadership approach built around the TLC Framework.

Ihab is now based in Vancouver, Canada and leads a team of coaches and personal development experts, providing services internationally to support in building a culture of leadership based on coaching.

Endnotes

1 Rosalynn Carter, former First Lady of the United States, in her book "First Lady from Plains," published in 1984.

2 Botelho, Elena, and Kim Powell. "Why CEOs Fail." Harvard Business Review, vol. 95, no. 7-8, 2017, pp. 76-85.

3 coachingfederation.org.

4 "Leaders Eat Last: Why Some Teams Pull Together and Others Don't," which was published in 2014 by Portfolio. The quote can be found on page 45 of the paperback edition.

5 Senge, P. M. (1990). The Fifth Discipline: The Art & Practice of The Learning Organization. Doubleday/Currency.

6 Lombardi, V. (1970). What it Takes to Be Number One. In H. J. Goldsmith (Ed.), Lombardi and Landry: How Two of Pro Football's Greatest Coaches Launched Their Legends and Changed the Game Forever (pp. 128-129). McGraw-Hill.

7 Goldsmith, M. (2007). What Got You Here Won't Get You There: How Successful People Become Even More Successful. Hyperion.

8 Sadhguru. (2018). Essential Qualities of Leadership. Isha Foundation.

9 Mandela, N. (1994). Long Walk to Freedom: The Autobiography of Nelson Mandela. Little, Brown and Company.

10 Norton, R. (2019). The Power of Starting Something Stupid: How to Crush Fear, Make Dreams Happen, and Live Without Regret. Shadow Mountain.

11 "Voltaire's Philosophical Dictionary" (1764), specifically in the article titled "Question."

12 Burton, J. P., Hoobler, J. M., & Scheuer, M. L. (2012). Moderators of the relationship between employee mood and organizational citizenship behaviors. Journal of Applied Psychology, 97(2), 391-403. https://doi.org/10.1037/a0025666.

13 Harter, J. K., Schmidt, F. L., & Hayes, T. L. (2002). Business-unit-level relationship between employee satisfaction, employee engagement, and business outcomes: A meta-analysis. Journal of Applied Psychology, 87(2), 268-279. doi: 10.1037/0021-9010.87.2.268.

14 Kok, B. E., Coffey, K. A., Cohn, M. A., Catalino, L. I., Vacharkulksemsuk, T., Algoe, S. B., Brantley, M., & Fredrickson, B. L. (2013). How positive emotions build physical health: perceived positive social connections account for the upward spiral between positive emotions and vagal tone. Psychological science, 24(7), 1123-1132.

15 Csikszentmihalyi, M. (1990). Flow: The psychology of optimal experience. Harper & Row.

16 Paraphrased from a larger passage from "Meditations" (Book VIII, 47).

17 Saint-Exupéry, Antoine de. The Little Prince. Translated by Katherine Woods, Harcourt, Brace and Company, 1943.

18 Brown, B. (2010). The gifts of imperfection: Let go of who you think you're supposed to be and embrace who you are. Center City, Minn: Hazelden.

ENDNOTES

19 Andersson, L. M., & Pearson, C. M. (1999). Tit for tat? The spiraling effect of incivility in the workplace. Academy of Management Review, 24(3), 452-471.
    Miner, K. N., & Eischeid, A. C. (2012). Workplace bullying and the risk of absenteeism. Journal of Occupational Health Psychology, 17(1), 91-95.

20 Fiset, J., Plante, A., & Cote, D. (2017). Social support at work and affective commitment to the organization: The moderating effect of job resource adequacy and ambient conditions. Journal of Occupational Health Psychology, 22(3), 371-382. doi:10.1037/ocp0000047.

21 Nelson, S. (2019). The Business of Friendship: Making the Most of Our Relationships Where We Spend Most of Our Time. BenBella Books.

22 Lao Tzu. (1997). Tao Te Ching: A New English Version. Translated by Stephen Mitchell. HarperCollins.

23 Gallup website in an article titled "State of the American Workplace" under the section "The Engagement-Performance Link: Getting Better Business Results through Engagement." The article was last updated on October 19, 2020. Here is the link to the article: https://www.gallup.com/workplace/238079/state-american-workplace-report-2017.aspx.

24 Lao Tzu, Tao Te Ching: A Book about the Way and the Power of the Way, translated by Ursula K. Le Guin, Shambhala, 1998, chapter 17, p. 80.

25 https://www.linkedin.com/pulse/jack-welch-just-shared-most-important-attribute-leadership-john-eades/.

26 Kennedy, J. F. (1961, January 20). Inaugural Address of President John F. Kennedy. Retrieved from https://www.jfklibrary.org/archives/other-resources/john-f-kennedy-speeches/inaugural-address-19610120.

27 "The Spirit to Serve: Marriott's Way" by J. W. Marriott Jr. and Kathi Ann Brown, published in 1997 by HarperBusiness.

28 Hill, N. (2008). Think and Grow Rich. Penguin.

29 Covey, S. R. (2006). The speed of trust: The one thing that changes everything. Simon and Schuster.

30 Zak, P. J. (2017). The neuroscience of trust. Harvard Business Review, 95(1), 84-90.

31 Brown, Brené. Daring Greatly: How the Courage to Be Vulnerable Transforms the Way We Live, Love, Parent, and Lead. Gotham Books, 2012.

32 Brown, B. (2013). The Power of Vulnerability: Teachings on Authenticity, Connection, and Courage. Sounds True.

33 Chris Bailey https://www.socialmediatoday.com/content/listening-what-isnt-said.

34 Stanley, A. (2011). Communicating for a Change: Seven Keys to Irresistible Communication. Multnomah.

www.ingramcontent.com/pod-product-compliance
Lightning Source LLC
Chambersburg PA
CBHW031105080526
44587CB00011B/841